MULTI-DIMENSIONAL LIFE

Also by Moyra Caldecott

FICTION
*Guardians of the Tall Stones:
The Tall Stones
The Temple of the Sun
Shadow on the Stones
The Silver Vortex*

*Weapons of the Wolfhound
The Eye of Callanish
The Lily and the Bull
The Tower and the Emerald
Etheldreda
Child of the Dark Star
Hatshepsut: Daughter of Amun
Akhenaten: Son of the Sun
Tutankhamun and the Daughter of Ra
The Ghost of Akhenaten
The Winged Man
The Waters of Sul
The Green Lady and the King of Shadows
Adventures by Leaf Light and Other Stories*

MYTHS AND LEGENDS
*Crystal Legends
Three Celtic Tales
Women in Celtic Myth
Myths of the Sacred Tree
Mythical Journeys, Legendary Quests*

POEMS
The Breathless Pause

AUTOBIOGRAPHY
Multi-Dimensional Life

BIOGRAPHY
Oliver Z.S. Caldecott

MULTI-DIMENSIONAL LIFE

Moyra Caldecott

Published by
Bladud Books

The front cover is from a pastel by Oliver Caldecott.

The picture on the back cover is "Eclipse of the Moon" by Oliver Caldecott, which is referred to on pages 141 and 105.

Copyright © 2007, Moyra Caldecott

Moyra Caldecott has asserted her right under the Copyright, Designs and Patents Act, 1988, to be identified as the Author of this work.

First published in 2007 by Bladud Books.

This Edition published in 2007 by Bladud Books, an imprint of Mushroom Publishing, Bath, BA1 4EB, United Kingdom

www.bladudbooks.com

All rights reserved. No part of this publication may be reproduced in any form or by any means without the prior written permission of the publisher.

ISBN 978-1-84319-549-8

Contents

Introduction		1
1	Bronze Age Britain	9
	I: *The Tall Stones*	11
	II: *The Temple of the Sun*	28
	III: *Shadow on the Stones*	38
	IV: *The Silver Vortex*	40
2	Bronze Age Crete	45
	The Lily and the Bull	45
3	Hebrides and Iceland in the Middle Ages	51
	I: *The Weapons of the Wolfhound*	51
	II: *The Eye of Callanish*	54
4	Space Fiction	57
	Child of the Dark Star	57
5	Dark Ages Britain	61
	The Tower and the Emerald	61
6	Eighteenth Dynasty Egypt	75
	I: *Akhenaten: Son of the Sun*	77
	II: *Hatshepsut: The Daughter Of Amun*	111
	III: *Tutankhamun and the Daughter of Ra*	132
	IV: *The Ghost of Akhenaten*	142
7	Anglo Saxon Britain (Seventh Century)	161
	Etheldreda	161
8	Stories of the West Country	175
	I: *The Green Lady and the King of Shadows*	175
	II: *The Winged Man*	181
	III: *The Waters of Sul / Aquae Sulis*	186
9	Non-fiction	197
10	Biography and Autobiography	199

Introduction

We live in a multi-dimensional Universe subject to multi-dimensional Time, and to try to record one day of one's life comprehensively is almost impossible.

I can say I was born on 1 June 1927, but what does that mean? Not only is the date subject to question because of the arbitrary nature of our dating system and the changes it has undergone through history, but what forces and events since the beginning of the Universe went into the drawing together of that particular sperm and that particular egg to bring me to birth on that day? In writing an autobiography should I therefore start only with my most recent ancestors? But several books could be written about one event alone in the lives of my paternal grandparents. What made them leave a comfortable life in Victorian England to emigrate to the wilds of Southern Africa in 1880? What hardships did they endure landing a few months after the bloody battle with the Zulus at Rorkes Drift? But even if I could write adequately about this one event, it would only be one thread in a complex weave of events, relationships, joys, fears, loves and hates that made up their day-to-day lives, and subsequently influenced me in my own reaction to the world.

In my novel, *The Tower and the Emerald* (chapter 9) I tried to express something of the complexity of every given moment. The heroine, Viviane, is being guided by a Celtic monk towards enlightenment. She is sitting quietly, watching a river.

> She listened to the birds... noted the sparkle of the water as it hurried over and between the rocks... the green of the bushes that hung over the far bank, some of them trailing branches in the water, continually buffeted...
> Then she began to listen to the water...
> She began to forget herself and hear only water sounds... complex... beautiful... a hundred different harmonies

within the same song. The water spoke, liquid-tongued, lightly lilting each tale a hundred different ways…

She could have listened forever… but Brendan's voice was calling her… cutting through…

'What have you learned?' he asked as she joined him.

'I have learned that there are many ways to tell everything that is to be told, and that man's language is clumsy and inadequate. It can tell only one tale at a time, and that tale only one way at a time.'

In this book I refer to the numinous incidents in my life several times, coming at them from different angles, illuminating them in different ways as I learn more through my progression as a writer.

The universe is not only made of matter, subject to the laws of physics, but is infinitely more subtle and complex, some levels of which we cannot even guess at, but which we know are in operation because we feel the effects. Consciousness is one of the most mysterious and powerful forces within it. Even if we distinguish between the three best known types of consciousness — the "sub-conscious" psychologists are so interested in; the "ordinary" consciousness we use to deal with the physical universe in our day to day lives; and the "Higher" Consciousness that we slip into in those moments of enlightenment when we seem to know more than we possibly can — we have not distinguished all the other levels and gradations of consciousness in existence… the consciousness of animals, insects, trees, plants, angels and all the denizens of the Otherworld, let alone the consciousness of the Mystery behind it all we call "God".

It is not an aberration that most of the world's teeming millions believe in some religion or other. It is a universal acknowledgement, however badly expressed, that we believe the universe is not only made of matter. Elaborate systems of gods and goddesses, angels, archangels, powers, thrones, devils and demons, saints and bodhisattvas are named and worshipped in an attempt to make sense of the feeling we have that there is more to the universe than the physical. There has to be more. Our experience tells us so. Our consciousness tells us so. But we cannot prove it with the limited criteria science has arbitrarily laid down for us. Nor can we prove it if our spiritual life hardens into dogma and from there into deceit.

We must always remember each event of our lives is not only taking place on the stage we see before us, but is part of a much greater drama we know very little about.

And Time? What makes us think there is only one type of time marching inexorably from the past, through the present, to the future, measured by reference to the relationship of earth and sun? I believe Time and reality are multi-dimensional and it is an impoverished life indeed lived only in one time and in only one reality.

Linear time is the one with which we are most familiar. Measuring this type of time has given our lives order and predictability. We mark birthdays and anniversaries. We make appointments. But it has constricted us and adds to our stresses and anxieties. Everything has to be fitted into the straight jacket of minutes and hours, weeks and months. And not everything can. Our bodies are subject to a more individual orchestration of time. Women talk of the biological clock when they realise they are getting too old to bear children, yet the menopause happens at different times to different women. One man of seventy climbs the Himalayas. Another of the same "clock" age can barely walk or remember. One child reaches puberty earlier or later than another.

I am told that over a period of seven years all the cells in our bodies die and are replaced. This means that as I am now, not a single physical cell in my body is the same as any I had when I left my mother's womb. Yet why am I convinced I am the same person? I feel there *must* be more to me than the cells in my body!

Memory is also not restricted by linear time. In memory an event that took hours or years can be re-experienced in the mind in a flash. It has a continuing dynamic, continually upgrading as new experiences occur, changing and moulding according to new understandings and new needs. It cannot be understood only as a chemical or electrical discharge in the brain because it is too creative. I feel it is other than purely physical reality.

In most of my novels I presuppose reincarnation not as a certainty but as a possibility, even a probability. Like three-dimensional chess this adds an exciting complexity to our experience of Time.

In my novel *The Ghost of Akhenaten* (chapter 1) Mary Brown comments on a picture of the universe taken by the cameras on board the Hubble telescope, suggesting another way we might get the impression we have lived before.

> 'We are just part of the choreography of that universe,' she says. 'We are, it is true, hurtling through space on the surface of a very small planet, but our consciousness is free of time and space. You can experience ancient Egypt as though it is present in your life now because you can see the bigger picture where everything that has ever happened still exists in some form. You are in a sense seeing two stars separated by millions of light years, simultaneously…'

Linear Time has no place in memory, nor has it in dreams.

Scientists tell us dreams occur in the few seconds when we are not fully asleep, or about to wake. And yet we have long and complex adventures in our dreams that seem to take hours, days and sometimes even years.

But our "subconscious" and our "Higher" Consciousness operate in our dreams. Things lurk in the subconscious for years, flowing like underground rivers in a complex cavern system. Some are temporarily blocked, only later to have their channels opened, while streams from other sources flow through and join at different places.

Our normal everyday consciousness is like water in a bucket on a conveyor belt of Linear Time — limited and constrained — neither aware of the dark streams that run through the subconscious, nor the great shining expanse of the ocean of the Higher Consciousness.

On the night of 19 January 2001, I was having a bad dream about searching and searching for the way home and at every point finding the way blocked or leading nowhere. I was getting frantic when my husband, Oliver, who died in 1989, appeared and said "Don't worry. You are not lost. You just don't know the way."

Our dreams are an extension of our lives into another kind of reality and time. Not only do we collect the flotsam and jetsam of the day and examine it from a new angle, but I am convinced we receive messages from other worlds, other realities.

Centuries ago the writings of Virgil were used as a form of divination. The seeker after wisdom would open the text at random and interpret what was written there as a personal message. I use whatever method I can to access the infinite, whether it be dream, or far-memory or opening a book at random...

One day in 1993, some years after my husband Oliver's death, I was feeling particularly nostalgic for him. I was in a second-hand bookshop in Queen's Square, Bath, where he and I had had a happy time some years before.

I was sitting down while my friend was looking for a book. I was tired and didn't want to get up. But across the room a book seemed to be 'calling' me. I couldn't see its title and at last, impatiently, I rose, crossed the room and took it off the shelf. Its title was *Hudibras*. 'What a coincidence', I thought, because I was at that time writing a novel about King Bladud (*The Winged Man*) whose father was called *Hudibras*. I bought the book and walked out of the shop.

Later, sitting on a bench beside Bath Abbey, I opened the book to the title page and realised it was not about the ancient legendary King Hudibras at all, but was a book about Oliver Cromwell and the civil war in England by Samuel Butler, published in 1744. Meditatively I let the book fall open and my eye caught the words:

> The news of Oliver's death being brought to those who were met to pray for him, Mr Peter Skerry stood up, and desired them not to be troubled: 'For (he said) this is good news... for being ascended into heaven... He will there intercede for us and be mindful of us on all occasions...'

It couldn't have been more appropriate for me to get this message at this time! I pondered how many time-lines had crossed to give me that message. The bookshop was one I had been to with Oliver years before when we were still living in London, only passing through Bath. I thought the book was about Hudibras, an ancient British king from the seventh or eighth century BC, about whom I was at that time writing, but it was about Oliver Cromwell millennia later and centuries before my own Oliver's death. I was sitting outside Bath Abbey built in the thirteenth century, before the time of Oliver Cromwell, but on the site of a place sacred to the ancient people of Britain, possibly a temple built by King Bladud (the son of Hudibras). I was poised at the moment of opening the book in a timeless place raised on a cat's cradle of time lines from different eras. Samuel Butler who wrote those words in the early eighteenth century could have had no idea what special message it would have for me, a woman in the late twentieth century. Good writing is always thus free from linear time — appropriate to every questing soul.

Medieval Christians under the guidance of Aquinas saw existence as a series of layers, almost like concentric spheres radiating from a central point — *"that point being Eternity conceived as an infinitely concentrated singularity"*. Present day scientists might claim this point as the point at which the Big Bang occurred which brought about the existence of the universe. (A mystical concept if ever I saw one!)

Eternity is not the same as Everlasting, but outside Time altogether. In it past, present and future are non-existent. We, as conscious spirit, have our essential being in that singularity. It thus may be possible in our lives, temporarily extended in Time and Space, to get a glimpse of what is in Eternity.

When my husband died I avoided asking him for help because I feared it would impede his progress in the Other World — might take him away from doing something else more important. And then I got a message 'loud and clear' reminding me that in the Other World there is no Time or Space. He does not have to come from somewhere else to attend to me — because he has never left, just changed.

Because we call it the other 'world' we think it is like this one — only insubstantial. Eternity, the After-life, has to be totally, unimaginably different. If we are to understand how God can be aware of every sparrow that falls, 'He' cannot be somewhere else looking on. He and the sparrow have to be simultaneously existent, outside Time and Space.

When people say they are living *only* in the present moment they are deceiving themselves. The present moment is made complex and magnificent by all the threads of multi-dimensional Time that are threaded through it. There is no *naked* present moment, except perhaps in Eternity.

One of the most important faculties of the human mind, *Imagination*, is the bridge between the Known and the Unknown. It flashes with images, metaphors and symbols that illuminate the deepest and the darkest secrets of Being.

Myths and legends are produced by the imagination when it is functioning at its most serious and profound level. The body is a finely tuned, immensely complex and efficient instrument, capable of experiencing much more that we commonly give it credit for — and one of its functions is at once to house the 'growing point' of the soul, and to protect it from the damage it might suffer if it were exposed to too much transcendent experience, too soon. The imagination tests out the ground beyond ourselves and allows us to explore the way ahead in symbolic form before we have to encounter it in reality. The imagination gives us myths and legends — those marvellous, subtle, complex vehicles of esoteric teaching — to prepare us for our future. In seeking their meaning we are meant to find the meaning of ourselves. (*Crystal Legends*, Introduction).

The greatest of the themes pursued by the Imagination through Mythic Time is the significant Inner Journey — the Quest of the Soul for Itself. One step could take seventy years or a split second. The Quest can be started when one is five years old, or eighty. It has nothing to do with Linear Time, yet is expressed in terms we are familiar with from Linear Time.

It takes various forms, and often the goal is reached in pursuit of something else.

In the ancient Irish tale of the Journey of Maeldun — the hero sets off to seek revenge for the killing of his father. After years of extraordinary testing adventures in rough seas and on strange islands, he meets the man who killed his father only to find that he has forgiven him, and so outgrown his need for revenge.

I did not realise it at the time, but during the writing of my books I was on a Quest. By mapping it now I hope I might make others aware of the complexity of every given moment, and encourage them to look out for signs and wonders in their own lives.

One

Bronze Age Britain

"Guardians of the Tall Stones"
which includes the trilogy:

The Tall Stones
The Temple of the Sun
Shadow on the Stones

The Silver Vortex (the sequel)

I believe that the Neolithic Stone Circles found throughout Britain formed a grid of spiritual energy which linked and sustained the isolated communities which existed in the Bronze Age. Their power could be manipulated by the well-intentioned, as well as the unscrupulous.

I: *The Tall Stones*

The Tall Stones is the first of four books. It is set in a small, isolated community in Bronze-Age Scotland. Threatened by the evil designs of Wardyke, a corrupt and ambitious priest, the village finds its only defence in the courage of Kyra, a young girl possessed of amazing psychic powers. In order to overcome Wardyke and break his hold, Kyra forces herself to enter the forbidden Sacred Stone Circle, the spiritual heart of her village, and to invoke the great powers of that mysterious place — powers which she does not understand and cannot control.

As a child I had various experiences which I suppose could be put under the general heading of 'psychic'. Moments of telepathy were not unusual for me, nor were sudden sensations of being distanced from my surroundings while powerful insights would come to me, well beyond my years. Sometimes I even felt I was slipping out of my body and could watch events from above. These last sensations (which I later was told were the beginnings of 'astral travel') I hated, for they were accompanied by panic that I would not be able to get back in and would die.

After those early years when the paranormal seemed normal to me, I embarked on a rigorous academic education which made me doubt everything that had happened. I enjoyed university and studied hard for degrees in English literature and philosophy, subsequently becoming a lecturer myself. In 1951 I married a very intelligent, rational man who had no time for 'fuzzy brained' thinking. Everything had to be proved scientifically or dismissed as nonsense or wishful thinking. Having grown up in South Africa and been sickened by the apartheid regime of the country, we emigrated to England in 1951 and there took part in many protests and rallies against oppression and injustice. We were also very active in the anti-nuclear movement.

We had three children and very little money, and everyday life was not easy. But after my thirty-sixth birthday I began to notice that I was still having those strange, inexplicable experiences I had as a child — and no matter how much I tried to explain them away with my rational mind, I could not. After some time my husband began to be less dismissive and gradually opened his mind to the possibility that there might be 'more things in heaven and earth'... He remained to the end of his days a wise observer supporting me in every way he could, while taking care not to take on any idea that seemed ridiculous to him after careful examination. For ten years he ran a publishing house, Wildwood House, with a friend, Dieter Pevsner, and published many books on complementary healing and alternative realities. Ideas excited him and he enjoyed exploring them, but he was always cautious of 'channelled' manuscripts. I remember he sometimes wore a badge that read: 'Just because I am dead, doesn't mean I'm smart.'

In my forties I suffered from severe and unstable angina and recovered dramatically and miraculously after sessions with Dennis Barrett, a spirit healer. This was perhaps a turning point for my husband — as it was for me.

When I was young I wrote a great deal without actually having enough experience of life to make any real contribution. I was driven by a most persistent desire to be a WRITER. It was not surprising therefore that all of my manuscripts were rejected. Looking back on it now I suspect I had to go through that frustration in order to learn how to write. Each manuscript was better than the last, but still the rejection slips came in. When my little daughter saw a fat packet come through the letter box, she asked me: 'Are you going to cry, Mummy?' I invariably did.

Finally, aged forty-seven, I gave up, burned my manuscripts and sold my typewriter. I experienced a wonderful feeling of release as though someone who had enslaved me had suddenly let me go. The burden of trying to be a WRITER had been taken from me. I could turn my attention to something easier.

And then on 23 July 1975 I had an experience that I can only describe as an initiation into what it really means to be a writer.

We were staying with our friends at Newton Hill, near Aberdeen in Scotland. I had angina at this time and was limited in the amount of physical activity I could manage. The pain that gripped my heart from time to time and the belief that at any time I could have a serious heart attack and die, heightened my awareness of everything around me and gave the life of my mind and spirit a daily intensity I had only had before in isolated visionary moments.

My daughter Rachel's Norwegian friend, Elizabeth, staying with us for the summer, wanted to go horse riding. We took her to stables near Dyce and left her there for a few hours. Exploring the district to kill time until we needed to fetch her, we came upon an ancient stone circle on the top of a hill. The tall stones, threaded liberally with quartz crystals, overlooked forests on one side, and the distant gleam of the sea on the other. Oliver at once started sketching and Rachel wandered off. I sat down in the circle, at first noticing only the plants, the bird calls, the landscape… and then my consciousness seemed to slip into another dimension — or time. It seemed to me I was part of an ongoing story. Invisible people were around me. I knew their names. I knew what they believed. I knew what they were doing.

When Oliver called me to leave I stared at him in bewilderment, struggling back to the twentieth century and my current persona.

When we returned to London I began to write my experience down. Rachel had picked up a little piece of granite lying within the circle and when I held it the story flowed almost without my having to think about it — as though the stone were transmitting in some way. When I put it aside I struggled for words. It became very important for me to record everything I had learned in the circle. I believed I was about to die and had been given a task by invisible beings that I must complete.

In fact I finished the first of the Quartet, *The Tall Stones*, in hospital, one long and lonely night after a heart attack. Years later, in 2007, I am still alive and the book is still in print.

My early novels had all been for adults, serious sociological studies about racial prejudice, dysfunctional families and pacifist issues. The last book I wrote, before I gave up, was for children, *The Weapons of the Wolfhound*. I had submitted it to be published and had almost forgotten it when it was accepted. It was my first published book and an advance copy of it was brought to me in hospital by Stratford and Leonie on 1 April 1976. I will never forget the joy of holding it in my hand for the first time.

Rex Collings was interested to see my next book and I think he expected it to be for children. But I wrote it as it came and it can be read at any age. In fact I did not care if it was published or not. Since then I have rarely written a story that does not spring from a passionate and disturbing encounter with the numinous, the supernatural, the spirit-realms, and I know the difference between the slow struggle of writing with my own everyday competence, and the times when my pen is running away with me in a desperate attempt to keep up with thoughts that seem to be pouring in from a higher realm. I would not say I was 'channelling' to another person's dictation, but rather responding to inspiration in a way that uses all the latent possibilities of my own extended consciousness.

The highest sages are at home in many realities, though none I think have ever penetrated to the Most High while still in this world. Most of us have moments when we slip from one reality to another. Some have bad experiences with regions below this one; others experience heights they never dreamed they were capable of. When we insist on the existence of only one reality (as most people do) and try to explain all our experiences in terms of that one reality, not only are we wasting our potential shamefully, but are in danger of becoming ill. *The Tall Stones* was the first story I wrote of any real significance. It came to me powerfully and strangely when I was not looking for it; it expressed things I didn't know I knew, and it wouldn't let me go.

My own experiences of other realities that I had previously been taught to dismiss as 'coincidence', 'hallucination', 'chance', etc. began to make sense as they were written down.

At first I was so excited to discover that I was right to believe that the life we have is multi-dimensional, that I rushed about sampling anything and everything that was connected with this 'other reality' — dowsing, astral travelling, telepathy, psychometry, mediumship...

And then I had a dream...

I was on a great ocean liner and we were expecting a visit from some Shining Beings from a Higher Realm. I was laying the table for the feast and excitedly helping myself to little portions from each of the bowls of delicious food I was carrying in from the galley. As a result I was violently sick and had to be put to bed, missing the visit of the Shining Beings altogether.

I knew when I woke that this was one of those 'teaching'

dreams that stay with you until you have understood its message fully. I remembered every detail vividly. I knew what it was saying. I gave up rushing around trying to sample any and every possible psychic experience, and concentrated on what seemed to me to be my task, the one my whole life had been a preparation for — the writing down in easy story form the insights I had received and was still receiving.

I was having the most amazing and relevant dreams, and when I opened a book at 'random', with a particular question in mind, I invariably received an answer. Friends and strangers fed me information in apparently unrelated conversations, and I frequently felt I was slipping in time and experiencing other lives. Thoughts and ideas and knowledge I had had for years seemed suddenly to join together to make a significant pattern. In a sense I wasn't learning anything new, but what I had known was being illuminated. It was as though I was looking at a familiar landscape for the thousandth time, but a sudden ray of sunlight lit up certain features showing their significance to me for the first time.

The angina made me almost an invalid, but I was living an active and adventurous life without ever leaving the house.

The one book grew into three, which have now been put together to form "Guardians of the Tall Stones". A sequel, *The Silver Vortex*, brought the number up to four. The story would still not leave me alone. Quilla, the young bull leaper in *The Tall Stones*, appeared again in *The Lily and the Bull* as an aged seer. My novel, *Daughter Of Amun*, set in Egypt, is about the female pharaoh Hatshepsut, but Kyra's daughter from the "Guardians of the Tall Stones" pursues her vocation as a priestess and a healer in that book too.

One of the things that has prompted me to believe that when I write these books I'm in touch with something beyond my ordinary self, is that I so often have confirmation after I have written something that it is indeed so.

Questioning why I had written so many 'yogic' ideas into Bronze Age Britain, particularly as the time I was writing about was probably before the time of the Vedas and the Upanishads, I read in the *Bhagavad-Gita* about *'an imperishable yoga... handed down... in succession, by the king-sages from ancient times and yet lost, by long lapse of time, and having to be retaught...'*

I believe in the cyclical nature of most things, including

knowledge. A Greek scientist, Aristarchus of Samos, taught in the third century BC that the earth and the planets moved round the sun, yet for centuries afterwards people denied it.

Kyra's experiences of spirit-travel, which in a fumbling and terrified way I had shared in my own life, I found described in *Tibetan Yoga and Secret Doctrine* by W.Y. Evans-Wentz (pub. OUP, 1935). *'The art of going out from the body, or of transferring the consciousness from the earth-plane to the after-death plane, or to any other plane, is still practised in Tibet, where it is known as Pho-wa'.* A reader of mine was shown a slab of stone in Australia by an aboriginal 'wise man', and told it was where the shaman in ancient times had prepared himself to leave his body so that he could spirit-travel to distant places.

I read about astral travel, which I had not read about before, and I had an experience of my own that was difficult to explain if it is not possible for the 'spirit' of someone to leave its body behind and 'travel'. One evening in May 1976 I was in a state of mystical excitement writing poem after poem on the meaning of the 'Fish' symbol in connection with Christ. Later I met a stranger who claimed I had appeared in her dream and prevented her committing suicide. 'But,' she said, 'why did you keep talking about fish?' It turned out it was exactly the time I had been writing those poems about Christ.

I was also very interested to read about Abaris, a priest of the Hyperboreans, described by Pindar, Herodotus, Pliny and Diodorus of Sicily, who visited Pythagoras, flying in on 'Apollo's golden arrow' and not eating anything the whole time he was with the community. No one knows where Hyperborea is, though the description of it fits Britain very well. If Abaris came from Britain by a kind of spirit-travel, to sojourn, learn and teach with Pythagoras, I wondered if the Pythagorian's belief in reincarnation and the indestructibility of the human spirit came about before or after the visit from Abaris?

The 'coincidences' of reading came thick and fast.

On the same day that I read in John Michell's *City of Revelation* that in the school of Pythagoras it was understood *'that each of the heavenly bodies resonates at a certain pitch, and the prevailing celestial harmony, varying according to the relative intervals between the planets, rings continually in our ears, imperceptible because we have never experienced its absence',* I also read in *Scientific American* (Special Issue: The Solar System):

Solar Song. When the earth is shaken by a large earthquake, the entire sphere rings like a huge bell (although the vibrations are much slower than audible sounds). It now seems that the sun vibrates in the same way...The oscillation (in the sun) that Hill and his colleagues have observed are believed to be the result of acoustic waves travelling back and forth inside the sun...

This reminded me of what I had already written in "Guardians of the Tall Stones":

The singing in their heads was the singing of the Spirit Spheres, the myriad realms of God, each voice, the full and separate syllable of each sound making up the secret name of God, only one letter of which was entrusted to each sphere, and our whole universe contained, with other universes, in only one of the spheres.

When I heard about the community of Findhorn in Scotland, which has had the most extraordinary relationship with plants, as Fern, one of my characters in the trilogy does, I opened a book about the derivation of place names, and found that Findhorn is a very ancient name, a remnant from a forgotten language which was in Britain before the Celts. The language of the people of the Tall Stones, perhaps?

When I wrote about sea urchin shells in Maal's collection of precious shamanic things, I had not read in Evan Hadingham's book: *Circles and Standing Stones* that: '*In a round barrow at Kellythorpe, near Scarborough, Yorkshire, a tall man was found shrouded in a cloak woven skilfully of nettle stems, fastened by amber buttons, accompanied by a bronze knife and wrist of guard made of polished stone and fastened with golden rivets. His body was ringed with sea urchins.*'

I had called my people 'the people of the Magus', 'Magus' being the name of their special star. I was not aware of why I called them this until I read, years later:

We think of the Magus as the possessor of occult secrets, a master of esoteric wisdom, who makes use of this knowledge for his own good as well as for that of his fellow man. He is a white magician, less fond of prodigies than of the contemplation of nature, in which he discovers marvellous active forces where others only see familiar things. For him the power of God is not concentrated in the One, but permeates every being of the universe. (Magic, Supernaturalism and Religion *by Kurt Seligmann, Pantheon Books, 1971.)*

I could not have wished for a neater summary of what I was fumbling to express in the trilogy.

Most of my books have been set in ancient times: "Guardians of the Tall Stones" and *Silver Vortex* in Bronze Age Britain c.1500 BC, *Daughter Of Amun, Son of the Sun*, and *Daughter of Ra* in ancient Egypt sometime between 1500 and 1300 BC, *The Lily and the Bull* set in Minoan Crete c.1600–c.1500 BC. *The Tower and the Emerald, The Green Lady and the King of Shadows*, and *Etheldreda* in Dark Ages Britain (AD 500–700). Only one has been set in the far future on another planet, *Child of the Dark Star*. But I never think of the period I'm writing about as a neat little parcel of time that has been left behind and that I am trying to recreate. I feel it is still with us. History is after all a map of waves, and the water in the ocean is always the same. We are ourselves present in the past and the future. I feel this very strongly though I know of no way of expressing it except through story.

My stories can be referenced to Linear Time c.1500–c.1450 BC — but are not limited by it. They can be referenced to the landscape of Britain, Egypt and Crete, but the protagonists are engaged on a spiritual journey that could take place anywhere.

When I write I always draw heavily on archetypal material.

The study of myth and legend has become a passion of mine. It seems to me these ancient stories, honed to perfection against the experiences of countless thousands of people, derive their layer upon layer of significance from their origin in the same reality I found myself in on that dramatic day in the stone circle. They use the diviner's trick of throwing a symbol of universal significance on to the table before us and letting us make of it what we can. The reason I prefer to express myself in story rather than in 'straight' prose is that I feel the realities of life are so intangible, so esoteric and mysterious, so delicate and subtle, that there is no way of conveying them directly. One has to see the meaning in flight like one sees the glance of light on a butterfly's wing. Pin the butterfly to a board and you have a pathetic shred of the original splendour. If that is enough for you, you will not bother to try to understand the truth that myths and legends embody. If it is not, you have an exciting time ahead with all time and space, and beyond, to play with.

An author, any author, will write into his or her book significant personal experiences, transforming them in the fictional version into something relevant to the characters and thus to a broader humanity. The process of writing fiction involves a continual exchange between the author's' own experience and the reach of his or her imagination — the Imagination being a creative act of extraordinary relevance to life.

To try to illustrate what I mean by this I will describe a few experiences of my own written into *The Tall Stones*.

I have already described how the book sprang from an experience I had in an ancient stone circle, near Dyce, Scotland on 23 July 1975. Sadly, in 1998 I had a card from friends near Dyce, telling me that the stone circle that inspired *The Tall Stones* is now in a loop of the access road to Dyce Airport and is no longer deep in the countryside as it was when I first encountered it. Were the ghosts of that ancient civilisation, aware that their sacred space was soon to be desecrated, anxious to get their story told before it was too late? I found it extraordinary that when I was wanting to research my book I hardly found any books on stone circles, but after 1976 they came pouring out from publishers and everyone seemed to be interested in them. 'Ancient Wisdom' from the Stone circles became a 'buzz' phrase for the New Age — which I hadn't even heard about when I had that experience at Dyce.

In the book, the young girl Kyra is initiated into the priesthood of her Bronze Age community, by the elderly, outgoing priest. A crucial part of her training is to show her how to control her "spirit-travelling" so that she might communicate with other priests across the world. Kyra's early experiments with out of body travelling are precisely based on my own.

The Tall Stones (chapter 3):

> Kyra said, "Well, one moment I was lying there just the same as usual and the next moment my *body* was lying there but somehow I was not in it."
>
> He raised his eyebrows.

"Were you in the place you saw when you were with Maal?"

"No. I was still here, in this Circle! I could see you as clearly as anything looking at the sea and some birds and not paying any attention to me, and I could see my body as clear as I could see you… only I was looking at it from *outside* and it looked dead. I tried to move my legs and arms but nothing would move. I tried to scream out to you but no sound would come. I even tried to open my eyes thinking that would make me wake up. But my eyelids would not move! And anyway I was not asleep. I really was awake, but I was not *in* my body."

"Are you sure you did not go anywhere else?" Karne asked, visibly disappointed.

"No!" she screamed. "You do not care about me at all! You just want your stupid questions answered. If I could not have returned to my body I would have *died!*"

"How did you get back?" Karne asked with interest.

"I do not know. I just tried and tried to get back in and suddenly there was a snap and I was in and everything was normal again except that I am never, *never* going to try that again!"

In 1974, '75 and '76 I often had those out of body experiences and I never enjoyed them. Three are particularly worth recording here I think. One afternoon I was lying on my bed resting because of the angina, and I "slipped out of my body". I remember thinking with relief that my son Julian would soon be back from school and he always called on me in my room to greet me. "When he does that", I thought, "it will trigger my return". I heard the front door open and he came clumping up the stairs. "Soon!" I thought. But for once he passed my room and went up to his own room without greeting me. I heard his door shut and his heavy school bag thump down on the floor. I was in despair — waiting for him, waiting to return to my body. Time passed. And then I heard the front door open, Julian clumping up the stairs, passing my room, shutting his own door and throwing his heavy school bag on the floor.

This time it was real, and the shock of realising that I had heard something in advance of it happening, snapped me back into my body.

A year after I experienced this I read a book called *The Astral Journey* by Herbert B Greenhouse. It described the phenomenon of out-of-body in great detail with many examples. The "arrival phantom" is evidently well known and called "vardogr" in Norway. According to Thorstein Wereide who writes about "Norway's Human Doubles" in *Tomorrow* magazine (winter 1955), the "vardogr" is heard as well as seen… there are steps on the stairs, the outside door is unlocked, boots kicked off. When the host investigates he finds the hall empty, but knows that his friend will soon be there.

The second also happened during the angina years when I was resting in an otherwise empty house. This time when I called out in terror someone kind and strong and comforting came into the room. "Strat," I thought, forgetting that my son Strat was in another town. He took hold of my shoulders on the bed, and as he touched me I snapped back into my body. There was no one there, and yet I had felt his touch physically on my shoulders.

The third was the last time I ever experienced this phenomenon. I described it in chapter 8 of *The Tall Stones*. During my own similar experience I prayed as I have never prayed before that it would not happen to me again. Later, when I read about astral travel and I wanted to experiment with it, I could not.

> But while they were having a happy time poor Kyra was in trouble again. She had managed to "travel" after a few false starts, but this time she found herself in a strange and horrifying situation. She was aware of her body lying on a beautiful golden couch but she was surrounded by a group of terrifying and hideous figures. Each had the body of a man clad only in a loin cloth that shone like metal, and each had the head of an animal, grinning and jeering and leering at her. She tried to get up but found she could not move her body. She tried to scream, but no sound would come from her throat. She realised she was outside her body again and had no control over it. She screamed and screamed, struggled and fought. She could *feel* herself doing all this, but she could see her body still lying there soundless and inert as though it were dead.

My experience in writing the book is something like the

game of leapfrog. I jump over an experience I have in everyday life to reach an imaginative transformation of it. Then I leapfrog over an imaginative event to reach an understanding of an event I had in my everyday life. Backwards and forwards I go between "everyday" and "fantasy", each illuminating the other, having a marvellous adventure while I learn about myself and about life, the story growing all the time exponentially!

In the novel, unlike me, Kyra went on to master spirit-travelling and became capable of visiting other countries. The countries she visited were based on countries I myself have visited either in real life, or in dream, or in study. I never myself visited them in just the way she did, though I believe such "travelling" is possible. The Yogi masters and sadhus of India, and even some western saints, have been known to appear in two places at once.

In *The Tall Stones*, Kyra travels to ancient Mycenae by identifying with Maal's memories. The cup decorated with bulls that she sees, I had seen in Athens Museum after my own visit to 'Agamemnon's palace in ruined Mycenae. It had stirred my thoughts in powerful ways then, and I knew I had to use it in one of my books. That someone could identify so closely with another's memories as Kyra did with Maal's does not seem impossible to me. A vivid and active imagination has helped me to approach this many times — no doubt aided by the power of telepathy.

Another experience Kyra had was based on a piece of labradorite I had that flashed with amazing coloured light from some angles, and an ancient stone sphere I had seen in a Scottish museum carved with concentric circles and spirals.

The Tall Stones (chapter 11):

> Tentatively and hesitatingly she put her two trembling
> hands forward and cupped them around the magical stone.
> The light within it seemed to go out and it felt like ordinary
> cold stone.
>> "Close your eyes." Maal spoke still with firm authority.
>> She closed her eyes.
>> "Feel the pattern of the stone with your fingers."
>> Delicately she moved her fingertips over the cold surface.
>> She felt the pattern.
>> "No. Do not open your eyes."

She was in a very dark darkness. It seemed darker within her head than it normally did when she closed her eyes. No images whatever came to her, not even those peculiar little wisps of shape that usually seemed to float upon the inside of her eyelids.

She could feel the icy ball of stone within the cup of her hands. Her fingers began to trace the spiral round and round the surface.

It seemed to have no end. Her finger tracing... the groove... the spiral... the sphere.

The spiral never left the sphere and yet never ended... as though the sphere and the spiral were eternal... She began to drift... to feel only the spiral groove going round and round the sphere until at last she lost consciousness of even her own finger in contact with it and was aware only of herself the spiral... herself the spiral...

In this state she was no longer aware of the darkness as darkness but as the night sky, immensely vast and filled with countless stars. When she had looked at the sky at night on other occasions she had seen the myriad sparks of light dotted about apparently at random. Now she was aware of it as an intricate but definite pattern.

She saw it as a pattern, each star linked with each other star in a relationship that was unmistakable. It was as though fine gold lines, as fine as spider's web, were drawn between each spot of light to make an exquisite network, complex and yet ultimately simple.

But even as she grasped this the vision was altering slightly. The web was not flat but had depth as well. The stars she had thought were all the same distance from her appeared now to vary, some nearer, some further away. The golden threads linked them not only sideways, but backward and forwards as well.

She felt herself moving nearer to them, somehow being among them so that the network of fine gold lines was around her in every direction... stars were around her in every direction.

As the sensation of movement grew she realised that it was not only herself that was moving. The stars, the golden lines, the darkness itself... everything was moving and everything was changing in relationship to everything else in subtle ways at every moment, and yet the overall web of relationship was still there… the threads never broke… only adjusted, stretched and altered.

In Chapter 15 of *The Tall Stones*, Kyra's visit to Bronze Age China is based on an extraordinarily vivid dream of my own, no doubt sparked off by a visit to the Chinese rooms in the British Museum.

Although most of the story and the characters in it sprang from my experiences in the Dyce Circle, while I was writing and rewriting it I was also reading and researching the Bronze Age, not only in Britain, but in the countries around the world I believed she had visited in spirit-travelling. I used what I learned, together with my own experiences in different contexts, to flesh it out. It seemed to me a pebble had been dropped into a pool when I stood in that Circle at Dyce, but the story also encompassed the ringed ripples that travelled out from it and which continued to feed me inspiration.

My husband and I visited Crete three times, and the magnificent Minoan civilisation held a particular fascination for me. Kyra spirit-travelled to it in *The Tall Stones* (chapter 15), meeting the bull-leaping acrobat, Quilla. In the same chapter she visited Egypt, another time and place with which I have always felt a strong connection. There she met the young priest Khuren who was to play such an important role in her life as a priestess.

There is no incontrovertible evidence that the ancient Britons had any communication with ancient Crete, though some authorities claim that an indentation on one of the tall stones of Stonehenge is in the shape of the Minoan double axe. Similarly there are speculations about the ancient British connection with Egypt because Egyptian faience necklaces have been found in Ireland and Somerset, and the remains of a boat off the east coast of England has been identified as the type used in ancient Egypt. T.W. Rolleston in his book *Myths and Legends of the Celtic Race,* mentions an Egyptian ankh carved on a stone chamber in Brittany.

But whether there was physical connection or not (and I can't see any reason why not) in the interplay of time and space that goes on in the human mind, the connection exists.

At Dyce I puzzled about the wide spread of the culture of

stone circles; I heard there are many hundreds known in Britain and Europe. Some have been found in Asia and Africa. I wondered how there could be such a homogenous culture over such vast distances at a time when the technology of travelling and communication was so primitive.

At that moment the idea of "spirit-travelling" came to me based on the stories I had heard about certain saints and sadhus being trained to leave the body.

Although I had never seen the great stone circle at Avebury in Wiltshire before I went to Dyce, I had heard of it. While I was writing *The Tall Stones* my friend Michael took me there and immediately I was overwhelmed by it. Touching the stones set up shivers in my spine and I knew that it must be one of the primary sacred temples of the culture I was writing about. These stone circles were already millennia old before Kyra's people lived, and many different cultures had lived and died in their shadow.

Kyra saw it first as a vision. In *The Tall Stones* (chapter 15) she spirit-travels there to meet the Lords of the Sun from across the World.

> Within the great Circle of Standing Stones she was aware of circles within circles of people moving rhythmically to the music of drum and flute, stepping sideways slowly and with elegance, their arms raised so that the tips of their fingers brushed their neighbours' as they moved. On a certain beat they dipped their heads and bent their knee in a way that gave the whole ring movement a sinuous serpentine character. As each concentric circle was moving around the Stone Circle in a direction opposite to the one within and without itself, the currents and eddies of invisible force generated were complex indeed.
>
> Undeniable forces and vibrations were set up, currents and eddies of power. She could feel it. She could almost see it. The pulsing of the music added to the intensity of the feeling. The mist that moved with its own serpentine life about their feet added to the impression of detachment from the earth. Everything was charged and potent. She was on a level of reality that she had not known before. Her heart began beating loudly. She had finally reached the conjunction of the Lords of the Sun.

In writing a novel one can play with ideas and concepts that hover on the edge of one's belief and, while doing so, consider seriously one's attitude to them.

At about this time I was reading a great deal about reincarnation, in the Hindu and Buddhist religions, and considering most seriously whether my own feelings of "having been there before" at Dyce, Avebury, Crete and Egypt could possibly be due to the fact that I had indeed lived there before. I am still puzzling about it — but more and more inclined to believe it. The fact that the ancient Celts who conquered and assimilated Kyra's people a few centuries after the book was set, also believed in reincarnation made me think I was not too far off the track.

Another idea I assimilated from my Hindu readings was the way certain sadhus could control their autonomic nervous system to such an extent that they could feign death, be buried alive, and recover. Maal, the shaman priest in *The Tall Stones*, prepares to control his own dying in a way that the Yogi masters of Tibet and India have been known to do.

> The message is, that the Art of Dying is quite important as the Art of Living (or of Coming into Birth), of which it is the complement and summation; that the future of being is dependent, perhaps entirely, upon a rightly controlled death…
>
> To those who had passed through the secret experiencing of pre-mortem death, right dying is initiation, conferring, as does the initiatory death-rite, the power to control consciously the process of death and regeneration…
>
> When Milarepa, Tibet's saintly master of Yoga, was preparing to die, he chose not only a favourable external environment… but an inner state of mental equilibrium in keeping with his approaching Nirvana. Indomitably controlling his body, which, having been poisoned by an enemy, was disease-weakened and pain-wracked, he welcomed death with a song, as being natural and inevitable.
>
> From the Preface of the second edition of *The Tibetan Book of the Dead*, translated by W.Y. Evans-Wentz.

That the ancient Celts also firewalked was an added incentive to link the two cultures in my mind. I'm not saying that the Bronze Age people of Britain were in physical contact with ancient India. But by humans being part of an interrelated whole, and by being basically so similar, it is not inconceivable that similar cultural practices will grow up across the world.

Certain things are universal to human kind. Religious aspiration is one, and its disintegration into superstition is another.

Many people today still take omens seriously. But what is an omen? Maal gives a good explanation in *The Tall Stones* (chapter 10):

> He wondered if she should tell her that omens are around us all the time. Everything is an omen if we choose to make it so. What makes an omen work is something in ourselves. We sense something from deep within us, on a level in which we are not used to being conscious, and we choose something from the "outside" world to project it on, to make it understandable for us. For instance, she would sense a need to take a journey, a readiness, a ripeness …and because she was not used to recognising such deep instinctual drives she would see a giant bird flying or a wind blowing a tree in a particular way and she would believe it was an omen telling her to go. She would think the message was coming from outside herself.
>
> If she saw the same bird flying, the same tree bending, when she was not ready to go, she would not see them as omens at all. It was another case of what was reality. The omens were real, but not in the sense the people believed them to be.
>
> He looked at her and decided she was not ready to recognise omens as part of herself. She had too much that was new already to cope with. It would be more comfortable for her to believe as most people believed, that omens were messages from the gods telling one what to do. Making decisions for oneself was always difficult and it was a sign of maturity when one could take responsibility for decisions. Kyra was maturing rapidly, but she was still a long way from this point.

II: *The Temple of the Sun*

Kyra, Karne and Fern undertake a long and hazardous journey to the Temple of the Sun (Avebury in Wiltshire) for Kyra to receive her training as priestess.

Almost as soon as I had finished *The Tall Stones* I started on its sequel *The Temple of the Sun*. The story would not leave me alone. I was living parallel lives as a middle aged mother of three, a semi-invalid with severe angina, and a woman of the Bronze Age having marvellous adventures across time and space. Each afternoon when my daughter Rachel came back from school I would read her what I had written and we shared the adventure. I hope it made up for the times she came back from school and found me lying, grey in face, and had to call an ambulance to take me to the hospital.

In *The Tall Stones* Kyra had developed from a carefree fourteen year old to a teenager on the verge of womanhood who had learned that she had a difficult responsibility to her community. To fulfil this she had to train as a priest. She, her brother Karne and his pregnant wife Fern, had to travel to the far south, across stormy seas and overland through dangerous forests to *the Temple of the Sun*, the centre of her people's religious aspirations. I call this temple "Haylken" in the book. The huge stone circle, still standing, is now called Avebury in Wiltshire.

On 5 April 1976, my husband Oliver, my son Strat and his wife, my daughter Rachel and I stayed in a cottage near Avebury for a few days. I had been writing *The Temple of the Sun* since early February and had almost finished the first draft, but I knew the beginning was not right. I have always had trouble with beginnings and endings, probably because there are no clear-cut beginnings and endings in life except in a superficial sense.

I could not walk very far without doubling up with pains in the chest, so I settled by one stone while the rest of my family explored further afield. I leant my forehead against the stone and kept very quiet. Thoughts began to come to me that felt like memory. I thought I saw a face, Guiron's face, very vividly, so vividly indeed that every time I shut my eyes that day I had an after image of it as though it was emblazoned on the inside of my eyelids.

I went back to the cottage that night, tore up the first few pages of the *The Temple of the Sun*, and replaced them with the following:

The High Priest, the Lord Guiron, was in the Great Circle of the Temple of the Sun by himself, the dawn rituals over, the other priests and initiates departed. He too should have left and be attending to the business of the Temple.

Something held him back.

Something made him break his routine and pace the Tall Stones around the circumference not as a priest drawing energy from them, not as a suppliant speaking with spirits, not as Lord of the Sun in robes of splendour with the power to roam the world at will, but as an old man suddenly lonely and afraid.

It was as though the people leaving the Circle after the Ceremony this particular morning drained him of his significance. He had not felt this way before, or not for many years. He had been in the Circle alone many times… as High Priest it was his Right, but it had always sustained him in his confidence and strength.

Now he felt like a peasant who had wandered unwittingly into a Sacred Circle and was overwhelmed by his own smallness and in awe of the Giant Forces surrounding him.

He, Guiron, Lord High Priest, was afraid.

Afraid in his own Temple?

Afraid of what?

He did not know.

The shoulders he usually carried so straight and proud were bent.

"What is it?" he kept asking himself.

But for all his knowledge of the Mysteries, and for all the control of Mind and Body he had learned through the long years of priesthood, this time he was an ordinary man faced with an uneasiness to which he could not put a name, which he could not define.

On the journey south Kyra's small group had many adventures. At one time they sojourned with villagers who were terrified of monsters in the forest. Kyra, realising that they were not real physical monsters, encouraged the villagers to make clay images of them and dissolve them away in the river. Eight years after I'd written this I read a passage in a book called *Survivals in belief among the Celts* by George Henderson: "A figure is made of clay... and placed in a stream on the principal that the sooner the clay-body dissolves, the sooner will the body of the person thus represented be destroyed."

In *The Temple of the Sun* (chapter 3) I wrote into the story my own feelings about The Rollright Stones in Oxfordshire. Because of my now passionate interest in stone circles I had been taken to Rollright. But I had had a very bad feeling about the place as though black magic had been practised there. We have to remember these circles have been in existence for thousands of years and whatever they were used for by their original architects in the Neolithic Age, might not be what they were used for in all those centuries since. At Dyce I had a good feeling. At Avebury also. But at Rollright I had a very bad, bad feeling. Again this might have been personal to me. Maybe something bad had happened to me there in a past life.

At Christmas 1975, Strat and Leonie who lived at Oxford, and, knowing that I had held a stone from Dyce to help me in my writing, and not knowing about my dread of Rollright, brought me a piece of stone they'd found lying in the circle. At that stage I was sleeping downstairs in the dining room of our big Victorian house because I couldn't get up the stairs to our bedroom. I went to sleep with the piece of rock from Rollright beside my bed. In the night I woke in a cold sweat with terror. It seemed to me the whole house was surrounded by demonic savages, shrieking imprecations and threats — trying to get in to me. (More than 20 years later this same nightmare experience was written in to my novel *The Ghost of Akhenaten*.)

In the morning I gave the stone back to my son and daughter-in-law and asked them to return it to Rollright. I did not want it in the house a moment longer.

Rollright itself has a legend that you cannot count the stones — you will always get a different number. There is also a legend that several outlying stones are humans turned to stone because they didn't go to the church on Sunday. I knew a lot of dark legends about stone circles have arisen since Christian times because the Church wanted to drive people away from worshipping their traditional gods, believing them to be devils. But I have rarely felt any unease in any other circle I have been in — though many of them have such legends. At Avebury itself there was a concerted effort to destroy the ancient temple; one farmer was called "Stone Killer Robinson" because he smashed up so many of the standing stones. The little church in the village of Avebury is built just outside the circle and the font has a carving of a dragon biting the foot of a bishop — a dire warning to the parishioners about the monstrous dangers of the old religion.

Some months before our family visit to Avebury my husband had written to Denis Barrett, a healer recommended by a friend in Bristol. We were at our wits end. I was having attack after attack of angina and most of the drugs I was taking from the hospital proved to have bad side effects. Oliver didn't really believe in spirit-healing, but he did respect the friend, Rebecca Hall, who recommended the healer to him. Barrett wrote to me and suggested I hold his letter at a particular time every night when he would beam healing energies at me. I did this for some time without much hope of success. But when I received a letter from him saying that my doctor would change my medication on a particular day, and my doctor did, I began to believe in him.

During the time I was writing *The Temple of the Sun* I had two visits to Bristol to see Mr Barrett. When my angina completely disappeared after the second of these visits, I was led to believe more than ever in the things I was writing about. Barrett said his spirit helpers were using ultrasonic waves on me to dispense the gunge around my arteries. He said doctors were not using this method yet, but would within 10 years. In 1988 a friend sent me an article in "The Lancet" claiming ultrasonic as the newly discovered method for cleaning arteries. I continued with renewed confidence to write about the spiritual and psychic dimension to life — not forgetting my own dramatic experience of healing.

From *The Temple of the Sun* (chapter 9):

The Winter passed in training for Healing.

They learned a great deal about the body and the natural ways it had of healing itself. They learned how the mind, clouded by fear and doubt, could hinder these natural ways, and how they, as priest-healers, could bring back confidence to the patient so that the ways of nature could work again freely.

It seemed the mental image a person held of himself had great power to influence his body. They were taught to change with great tact and skill the self image of illness the patient held tenaciously within his mind, to one of well being and health. The image changed, the patient visualising himself well, the healer's work was done. Nature did the rest.

They learned that when the illness had gone too far for the patient's own body to heal itself, they could transfer the strength of their own life-force, to aid the natural healing processes within the patient.

They learned to do this by laying their hands upon the sufferer and directly "willing" the strength which they knew flowed through them from the Great Source of Life, to enter his body and make him whole again, to by-pass, to push aside, the impediment within the patient that was preventing his natural supply of life-force from entering.

They also learned to use the power of thought to do the same thing when they were too distant from the sufferer to touch him physically. They studied how to prevent illness, what to eat and how to exercise. The movements they practised were always simple, slow and effective, control of body built up gradually stage by stage until it became a perfect instrument for the use of its owner on earth.

In Kyra's training I incorporated much of what I had myself learned, about healing, divination, prediction and prophecy.

The first thing Kyra learned in the class for divination was that the power of divining was not in the object itself, but in the mind of the "Seer," so that it was perfectly in order for them to use anything they liked as aids to divination.

And with prediction she learned that,

...it is not only the present life of the man who asks for help that you must consider, not only what he *thinks* he knows about himself. You must search the inner levels of his mind and reach the real Self he might not even recognise. The time scale you must use must be as long as Time itself. He does not come into existence with his birth, nor leave it at his death. Remember this at all times.

The Temple of the Stones (chapter 9)

When Kyra learned to project images telepathically into other peoples' dreams I was thinking of the time a friend and I carried out such an experiment and had success. He was driving to the South of France in a mini car with his son and daughter uncomfortably squashed in the back seat trying to sleep with the rain beating on the metal roof. Back in London I dreamed of trying to get all my furniture into the small garden shed in a downpour. The next night he nearly drove over a black cat — and I dreamed of a witch and her cat.

In chapter 5 I dealt with my ideas on Thought:

Not only in the "Silence", but all the time, whether she knew it or not, she was influencing with the flow of her thought people outside herself, and they were influencing her.

Thought became more than just the rambling monologue she was accustomed to hearing within her head.

It became a Force that she respected, a force that perhaps had shaped the Universe in the first place, but certainly shaped the day to day existence of all around her.

Also in chapter 5 of *The Temple of the Sun*, I wrote one of my own visionary dreams into the text as though it had happened to Kyra. Again — leap frogging from my life to Kyra's and back again! In *my* dream I was witnessing the invasion of Tibet by the Chinese.

Kyra woke remembering the utter desolation that had once been the most magnificent civilisation she could ever have imagined.

The class listened spell-bound to her story. It was a message from the spirit realm. Of that there was no doubt in their minds. None of these things had ever happened to

Kyra in this life, and there were things in the dream that she could not have known about or seen.

After a long silence the teacher said to Kyra,

"What have you learned from this?"

They all knew that with spirit messages you always took the meaning that came to you at the moment of waking. This was part of the message.

They never discussed, or analysed, these kind of dreams even if the interpretation that came with them seemed at first illogical.

"I learned that nothing is ever completely destroyed, but lives on, in another form. What is past nourishes what is present, and what is present nourishes what is future, and there is no changing this.

"And I learned that the Temple I saw was not only in the future, but was also in the past. This had all happened before and would happen again. The Circle and the Spiral are the most potent symbols of Being known to man.

"The Seven men of Wisdom, the Guardians of the Mysteries, rescued the seed pod rather than any of the fabulous paintings or scrolls of writing, because it contained the germ of Life that would grow again wherever it landed into another civilisation. This one was finished, but a new one could grow as long as this Mysterious seed containing spirit-force was preserved.

"I realised this world, or any other world, could have had many such civilisations which had disappeared and grown again, as it were, from seed.

"And we who grow do not remember the others, no more than the seed remembers the tree from which it was taken, or the tree remembers the seed from which it grew. But the tree would not be what it is if it had not come from such a seed. And the seed would not be what *it* is had it not come from such a tree."

When I started writing about Kyra's training in dream interpretation I was just wondering whether in the Bronze Age they would have such sophisticated techniques of psycho-analysis, when I was given the book *The Roots of Consciousness* by Jeffrey Mishlove (Random House & Bookworks, Berkeley 1975). There I read:

The Senoi live in an isolated rain forest in the Central Range of the Malay Peninsular. They claim to have lived for two or three centuries without violent crime, armed conflict, or mental and physical diseases. They attribute the alleged high degree of psychological integration and emotional maturity to the insight of their healers and teachers. Dream interpretation is a regular feature of their education and daily social intercourse.

> (Mishlove takes this from Kilton Stewart, "Dream theory in Malaya" in *Altered States of Consciousness*, ed. by Charles T. Tart, Doubleday, New York, 1972)

Before I was so miraculously healed of angina I had spent a long sleepless night in an upstairs ward of St Thomas's Hospital, London. My local hospital was Kings College in Camberwell, but because there was some kind of strike I was taken to St Thomas's that night instead. I lay all night watching one star cross the sky through the clear plate glass window. The thoughts that came to me that night I wrote into *The Temple of the Sun*, chapter 8. If I had gone to Kings College Hospital I would not have been able to watch that star or have that experience.

On a clear, moonless and cloudless night, she entered the great Stone Circle of the Temple and lay upon her back on the grass, her feet towards the East where the Sun would rise.

She was alone and the whole night was hers.

This night she must not let her attention wander for an instant.

The Star the High Priest had chosen for her was rising at the moment she lay down and she must watch its progress across the sky, unwaveringly the whole night long. No matter how tired her eyes became she must not let it out of her sight for an instant.

The effect of the high earthen ridge around the Circumference was to cut out all sight of the landscape and the villages around. She was isolated in a Circle of Power in complete darkness, alone with the Stars.

As the night progressed she totally forgot herself lying on the grass. All that existed was the one star she followed, brilliantly in focus, while an incredible pattern of subtly changing points of gold moved round in the background of her vision.

The star she watched not only moved with slow but inexorable majesty across the dark forever hole of the night sky, but grew in brightness and in power until she felt it like a sharp needle point actually penetrating the centre of her forehead.

It seemed to her the earth bank and the Tall Stones surrounding her not only kept the rest of the world out, but concentrated the power of the stars and whatever realms of Reality that lay beyond her normal consciousness, until they grew in strength and became the only Reality of which she was aware.

"The Field of the Grey Gods" that I describe in *The Temple of the Sun* is based on the field of loose grey sarsen stones that is near The Ridgeway, that passes Avebury. The Ridgeway is one of the oldest roads in Britain and certainly existed in the Bronze Age, probably even in the Neolithic Age. These stones lie about on the surface, probably brought down by great glaciers of ice in the Ice Age. Most of the gigantic stones at Stonehenge and Avebury are taken from here. I have never actually been to see these fields of stones, but I wrote them into my story because I'd heard of them and seen pictures of them. As far as I knew I had invented the stone that looked like an ancient throne and which had an extraordinary effect on anyone who sat on it.

Some years after the books had been published I met a couple at Avebury who, when they heard I had written *The Temple of the Sun*, which they had loved, said excitedly: "We found the throne in the Field of Grey Gods!" There was an actual stone chair there exactly as I had imagined it!

In the early 1990s I twice accompanied a party of Americans to Stonehenge at night. The leader of the group had permission for us to stay in the circle from 3 a.m. until dawn, although during these years Stonehenge was fenced off and carefully guarded. The first time was on 12 June 1992 in summer, the second at the equinox on 21 September 1993. Both were magical and significant experiences.

In *The Temple of the Sun* I call Stonehenge "The College of Star Studies". Here is an extract from chapter 7:

As the words finished issuing from the mouth of the High Priest, all the spectators found themselves singing, starting with a hum, the sound rising and rising until it seemed to reach the highest point of the sky where the last star flicked out as their eyes followed the sound upwards towards it.

And then the sound burst, and from hundreds of throats the hymn to the dawn on Midsummer's Day rose and spread outwards until the whole landscape was in light and sound, even the sombre burial mounds that ringed the Temple at a discreet distance transformed to something beautiful and joyful.

The air was suddenly full of birds, flying and swooping and arcing in time with the hymn.

Kyra was moved to tears. She wished the moment could last forever. She felt great thoughts within her, great feelings of wanting to help the world, to lift all human spirits up to join in light and love and absolute understanding.

In September it was raining hard when we entered the Stonehenge circle at 3 a.m. Fog lay close around the Stones, walling us in. I looked up, and the sky above the circle was totally clear, and the stars blazed down on me through a tunnel of fog. I was isolated from the rest of the world — experiencing the stars directly. I was Kyra. I was Moyra. I was Nameless in a mighty universe.

My own experience at Stonehenge, so many years after I had written the book, was for me another case of a profoundly imaginative experience giving me a taste of an experience that had happened in the past and would happen in the future. In other words, an experience in multi-dimensional Time.

III: *Shadow on the Stones*

Kyra and her Egyptian husband have to do battle to protect the Temple of the Sun and their society against the dark religion of the god Groth that is spreading through the country.

There is not so much to say about my writing of *Shadow on the Stones*, the first draft of which I finished in December 1976. As before, my interest in the characters I had first "met" at Dyce drove me on. Perhaps I started this one with more of a conscious interest in showing that the links formed in past lives do not always run smoothly in this life, and that religion, which can bring about the greatest good in the world, can also bring about the greatest evil. The misuse of privileges and power is a theme I continually return to in my books from Wardyke in *The Tall Stones* to Idoc in *The Tower and the Emerald*.

Shadow on the Stones is a shorter, darker book than the others in the series though it ends on a positive note. The Temple of the Sun is threatened by a rival religion with a fearsome god demanding blind obedience and sacrifice. Many such religions spring to mind from the Incas in Peru, to the Christian Church at some periods in its history, to the fundamentalist Islamic terrorists of today. The menace is fought in several ways — by Karne's warriors, by Isar's use of psychology, and by the Temple's own pure and selfless devotion to the Higher Consciousness.

Not much of my own experience came into this book except my hatred of a misguided, cruel and demanding religion that demands ignorance and blindness from its followers. The one surprising gimmick is the use of hang gliders in the Bronze Age. This idea came to me watching hang gliders taking off from a grassy ridge one day and realising how nothing in their construction could *not* have been reproduced before the technological age. This idea was further fortified by reading within twenty-four hours about Chinese manned kites from centuries ago, and the Nazca lines in Peru which are vast drawings in the desert which could not have been viewed properly except from the air. In my home town of Bath there is a legend from the late Bronze Age about a king who flew: King Bladud, father of King Lear. I later wrote a whole novel about him called *The Winged Man*. From Malmesbury, not far from Bath, there is a story of a monk who flew in the Middle Ages. The Celts have a story of Druid Mog Ruith who, in his feathered robes, "*rose up in company with the fire, into the air and the heavens*". (Anne Ross, *The Pagan Celts*, p.114, 115). The Greeks and Minoans also had their flying men — Icarus who failed and Daedalus who succeeded.

Not long after my book was published a friend told me he had seen a notice board on a hill in Wiltshire:

PRIVATE LAND
No hang gliding except by Flying Druids.

Whether this came before or after my book I couldn't tell!

IV: *The Silver Vortex*

Kyra's teenage daughter, Deva, plays with the dark side of magic and almost destroys the Temple of the Sun.

I did not return to the story of Kyra in earnest until February 1985. However, it had not been out of my mind completely. The novel that followed *Shadow on the Stones* was *The Lily and the Bull*, set in Bronze Age Minoan Crete.

By 1985, Arrow was publishing my books in paperback. I had written *The Tower and the Emerald* specifically for them and then they had republished my "Tall Stones Trilogy", now in one volume called "Guardians of the Tall Stones". I suggested that I write a sequel as the story was very much alive in my mind, and I wanted to know what had happened to the characters after the end of *Shadow on the Stones*. My editor at Arrow agreed, and I started writing *The Silver Vortex*. Actually it was provisionally called "Heir of the Ghost Owl"!

Bronze Age Britain (*circa* 1500 BC) and ancient Egypt came together again. Deva, the daughter of the British Kyra and the Egyptian Khu-ren, was growing up confused and restless in the community of *The Temple of the Sun*, haunted by memories of her past life in Egypt and resentful of the constrictions on her life as the daughter of two such powerful priests. She was easy game for Urak, a practitioner of dark and destructive magic.

As usual I fed into the minds of characters the things that were puzzling to me about existence, my own visions, temptations and failures. For instance, in chapter 16 of *The Silver Vortex*:

> 'What is it? Why do you look at me like that?' were the last words Deva said before Urak and Boggoron together pushed her over the lip and into the cauldron of boiling, icy water hundreds of feet below.

'This is my death,' thought Deva as she fell, and a strange calm came over her. There was the moment of terror — the scream that ricocheted against the dark rock, that pierced every nook and cranny, that battered itself against the walls like a bird caught in a chamber. But then everything went silent. She could not even hear the roar and the rumble of the water that was rushing up to meet her. The water was rushing, but she was still. She seemed to float, motionless, poised for a long, long, time above a terrible beauty. The liquid had become light… silver and diamond drops whirled in a spiral dance… filaments of gold spun and twirled… aquamarine, emerald, sapphire — all the jewels she had dreamed of — were spinning in this mighty silver vortex and she was going to become part of it. The walls of rock had completely disappeared now. She was in a world of white and silver spray. As though it was her own choice — like a salmon choosing the moment and the angle of his leap — she aimed at the centre of the whirlpool and was caught instantly in the powerful downward tug, the violent thirsty swallow of an ancient force…

As her head hit the solid muscle of the water she lost consciousness.

From above, Urak and Boggoron saw her whirling like a fragile black twig for a few moments and then disappear.

[…]

Suddenly the guide from the Hall of Records with the cold eyes, Wardyke, appeared.

'Am I dead?' she asked.

'No,' he said. 'You have come here to learn about the nature of matter — and the nature of will and thought. You are in the vortex of energy out of which a million worlds have been created. There is nothing here but pulses of energy — you may shape them into whatever you wish.'

[…]

She was tremendously excited. It was as though the universe was hers and she could mould it in any way she wished. Images of how she would like things to be if she had the power came to her mind — and with them came the urge to sing. She found herself uttering high, strange sounds, unlike any she had ever made before. Astonished, she noticed that the pulses of energy in the vast darkness were coming together and forming into objects. Her ideas were beginning to take shape. It was as though she were singing and thinking a universe into being. She remembered how Urak had recently shown her a piece of hide stretched tight between pegs and covered with a layer of fine dry sand. Boggoron and the old woman had been sitting on either side, chanting something — something that grew louder and louder until Deva had had to put her hands over her ears. She had noticed how the skin began to vibrate and that, as it did so, the sand shook on its surface and somehow formed into a geometric pattern.

Was this it? was this the key to manifestation-magic — sound causing vibrations which altered the pattern of the vibrations inherent in an object?

[...]

But suddenly she was afraid. Things were happening too fast. She could no longer control her thoughts or the sounds that she was making. Terrible, fearful ideas were coming to her and terrible, fearful things were coming into being. The more frightened she became, the more her thoughts raced about and the faster the world became peopled with monstrous and misshapen forms. The song she was singing had become ugly and discordant — each note worse than the last — and she could not think how to stop it and start again.

[...]

At that moment she noticed that Wardyke, who had been watching her with gloating satisfaction, fell back a step with an angry and startled exclamation. He seemed to dissolve before her eyes and then re-form into the figure of Maal. Beside him, and hand in hand with him, was the image of her mother. They both lifted their free hands to her head, and it seemed to her a beam of light was coming down from above, passing through their hands and into her head. In that light she saw clearly the dangers of what she and Urak were playing with. Create one thing, change one thing, and, however minutely, everything else had to change to accommodate it. The Unknown One who had created the universe could take into account the repercussions to the millionth, billionth degree — but their own limited minds could never encompass such a vast, complex and subtle design.

And then, suddenly, it seemed as though Time that had stopped, had started again where it had left off.

Deva heard a roaring in her ears and felt herself buffeted in the tremendous force of the whirlpool. She fought to stay afloat, catching a glimpse for a moment of the faces of Urak and Boggoron looking down at her. Then they were gone...

I had for some time been interested in the Kabbalah Tree of Life and had read several books on the subject, mostly by one Z'ev Shimon Halevi (Warren Kenton). In March 1983 I started attending lectures by him, and, although I never worked hard enough to master all the intricacies of the teaching, I gained enough insight for it to fire my imagination. In *The Tower and the Emerald* Viviane saw a vision of it when she was training to meditate at the monastery of the Fish, and in *The Silver Vortex* (chapter 11) I describe another vision of it:

From the forehead of each Lord of the Sun a narrow beam of brilliant light projected, and where they met in the centre of the circle was a vision so magnificent none of the candidates would ever be able to forget it, nor would they ever be able to describe it. It was as though they saw in one marvellous moment the beauty and the harmony of the whole of existence represented in a kind of living, vibrant Tree of spheres that was growing at once upward and downward, rooted in realms so high no one had ever penetrated their mysteries, its trunk bearing branches shimmering with life, reaching down till they brushed the earth ...while simultaneously it was rooted in earth and reaching up through all the green and growing spheres to the high realms of the Shining Spirits and beyond. There was a continual flow through trunk and branch and root. No part was left without change and movement and a meaning — from the gigantic stars on their majestic and ordered courses to the minutest component of the tiniest most primitive cell. Each had its place and purpose. Each contributed and was essential to the Whole.

They felt faint with awe. This was theirs. All this was theirs! They, as human beings, had the gift of consciousness beyond all others in the earth-realm to glimpse such reality. They could no longer justify any action they might take that did not take this vision into account.

They bowed their heads, and as they did so they felt the High Priest's finger upon their forehead and knew that the vision had been sealed in.

Deva eventually almost brought about the destruction of the Temple of the Sun by using manifestation magic to flood the community with luxury goods. This roused the ugly spectre of greed and envy. Raiders attacked and Kyra was killed.

I was thinking when I wrote this of the monasteries on Lindisfarne and Iona which were destroyed by the Viking raider seeking gold and jewels. If the monasteries had kept to Christ's teaching of poverty, they would not have been targets for attack.

Deva in horror, realising at last what she has done, set off for Egypt where she was to do penance and learn to be a healer.

When I came to write *Hatshepsut: Daughter of Amun*, I couldn't resist writing Deva, under her Egyptian name of Anhai, a "fictional" character, into the story of historical characters. She had become so real to me; I needed to know what happened to her.

Two

Bronze Age Crete

The Lily and the Bull

The Minoan civilization, one of the greatest the world has known, suddenly and mysteriously came to an end sometime during the period 1600-1450 BC, baffling present day historians and archaeologists alike. One of the most persistent theories is that it was fatally damaged by the immense volcanic eruption on the nearby island of Thera (Santorini).

This story charts the dramatic events during the last days of Ma-ii, a city on the north coast of Crete.

I have reworked *The Lily and the Bull* three times. It was first published in the UK by Rex Collings and in the United States by Hill and Wang, as hardback. When Corgi published it as paperback they wanted me to change my name. The WH Smiths chain of bookshops had not taken my "Tall Stones" series and the publishers wanted to pass me off as a new writer. Unwillingly I agreed, because I wanted the book to continue in existence. I have since very much regretted it — particularly as WH Smiths still didn't take it, and the readers who had liked my

"Tall Stones" missed out on it because they didn't know it was by the same author.

My son Julian suggested "Iskander Ben Zerffi", but I settled for a boring compromise, "Olivia Brown". "Olivia" because my husband was Oliver, and Brown because it was my maiden name. I felt it was important I kept some connection with my life.

For the paperback I rewrote bits of the story, and again when it was to be published as an e-book by Mushroom Publishing. The essentials have remained the same.

A book is never finished. It is never a satisfactory expression of one's original vision. I could rewrite every book I've ever written a dozen times and never be satisfied.

To celebrate my miraculous recovery from angina and the joy of having my books published at last, Oliver and I went to Crete from 22 April to 6 May 1977. Spring — the time of flowers! We stayed at a small guesthouse at the edge of the water just outside Aghios Nikolas. Sadly it is no longer there. At breakfast we sat under tamarisk trees and watched starfish in the crystal clear water of the bay at our feet. At night we watched the moon and stars over the distant mountains from our bed.

On 26 and 28 April we drove to Mallia along the old road. I felt strange, as though I had been there before. I wandered into the fields surrounding the palace and settled to contemplation in the ruins of a house. I felt very strongly that I knew how it had looked when it was inhabited in Minoan times. I 'saw' the wall paintings, the garden, the furniture, the people. I 'felt' the life all around me.

Much later, back in London, a friend lent me a book about Crete that had been published only in America. There I saw 'my' house described for the first time, and the wall paintings — the scraps of which the archaeologists had found — were as I had seen them in my mind.

On 29 April my "Tall Stones" was published. The encouragement this gave to my creative urge bore fruit in the ease with which the story of *The Lily and the Bull* came to me. By 3 May I was 'living' the story, and everywhere I looked in Crete I saw nothing of 1977 AD — but everything of *c.*1500 BC.

On our return to London we were plunged into worries about Oliver's and Strat's work situations, and I couldn't settle to writing at once.

But by August 1977 I was in full swing. One early morning I

woke to an overwhelming feeling of danger. I started writing, driven by something that was happening in my subconscious. I scarcely knew what I was writing. When I read it through after the emotional storm had passed I realised I had written about the flight of my characters from the Mallian plains to the mountains, shaken by earthquakes and threatened by a huge black cloud from the eruption of Thera eighty miles away. I had described the devastation of the tidal wave (tsunami) that struck the Cretan north coast at this time, my own feelings of terror as I wrote seemingly more than imagination.

A few hours later I was watching the news on television and learned that at the very time I was 'experiencing' the horrors of tsunami, a real tsunami was devastating an area of Indonesia. I must have been picking up the terror of the people trying to flee from it, telepathically, and that was helping me to understand what it must have been like in Minoan Crete when Thera erupted.

I learned years later that archaeologists had found that long after the sudden demise of the Minoan civilisation, pockets of Minoan culture survived in the mountains and the high plateau behind them, as I had described.

As always when I write a novel, the story is woven from many threads — some from academic research, but others from dreams, psychic events and real-life memories of my own. The battle between the two bulls in *The Lily and the Bull* (chapter 1) is based on a real battle between two bulls I witnessed as a child in 1936 on a farm in the Underberg, Natal, South Africa:

> He leapt up onto the wall and looked down into the dusty pen where the two giant bulls were tearing each other to pieces. The most valuable bull of all, the Black Thunderer, the one chosen by Queen Nya-an for the funeral of her son, was covered with blood and dust and frothing sweat.
>
> The earth shook as the two beasts pulled apart, turned, and charged at each other again and again. Red dust filled the air and Thyloss felt himself choking on it. Dimly he was aware of a group of children sitting in a row on the wall gleefully yelling encouragement to one bull or the other. They were not worried. It was a grand spectacle for them, and they cared nothing for the adult world of ritual and ceremony.

> Several terrified youths were darting about the enclosure with long pronged rods trying to prize the two apart, or at least to distract them. The high-pitched warbling whistles that were customarily used to guide the bulls added to the noisy turbulence, but had no effect on the enraged contestants.
>
> Thyloss could see that Grey Wind's eyes were red as he turned for another attack. He was not as fine a bull as the Black Thunderer, his coat was not so silky nor his horns so white, but his powerful build was reminiscent of the rocky strength of the southern mountains from whence he came, and he was not going to give in.
>
> [...]
>
> Grey Wind stood still at first, breathing heavily, froth dripping from his jaw. Suddenly he turned and lumbered off, trying to find his way out. In the confusion he missed the gate and stumbled into the wall where the children were sitting. Feeling the stone wall smashing into his nose, he roared and snorted, his muscles rippling in preparation for the attack on this new enemy. Feeling his hot breath on their legs, and seeing his red eyes so close, the children squealed and fell backward off the wall, a wriggling mass of arms and legs in the muck of the neighbouring empty bull pen.

The characters in the "Tall Stones" trilogy had become so real for me that it seemed to me they had taken on a life outside the pages of those books. When I was in Crete I kept thinking about the young bull leaper Quilla in the "Tall Stones", who had come from Minoan Crete. I felt her presence strongly on more than one occasion. But now she was old — a wise Seer living in the mountains.

Volcanoes have always held a particular and terrifying fascination for me, and many of my worst nightmares have been connected with them. Neither country I have lived in has any history of recent volcano or earthquake activity, and yet such activity seems to be part of my stored memory.

If my 'slip in time' was a genuine one in Crete, it may be that this is where these 'memories' and feelings come from.

From 6–20 September 1990 I was on the island of Santorini, ancient Thera, with a group from Bristol University and studied the evidence of that Bronze Age eruption I had described in

The Lily and the Bull. Many scholars date the disappearance of the great Minoan civilisation to the clouds of heavy dust, the earthquakes and the tsunamis that must have accompanied the eruption of Thera *c.*1600–1500 BC. Some say Plato's "Atlantis" was about this civilisation and this event. As I picked up pumice on the beaches of Crete, and saw the reach of the devastation of such eruptions as Mount St. Helens recently in the United States, I have no doubt that the 80 miles that divide Crete and Santorini from each other are of no account when such a gigantic event takes place.

On Santorini I walked among the archaeological digs at Akrotiri and saw the Minoan culture disinterred from its long sleep. I stared at the cliffs, layer upon layer of volcanic material. I explored the fumeroles of the active volcano still at the centre of the ancient crater. I picked up a piece of dark grey lava rock with the imprint of olive leaves still on it. Time slipped again and I was back on that fateful day when that olive tree was overwhelmed by a lava flow and one of the greatest civilisations of the world ceased to be...

In early March 1977 I gathered round pebbles on a beach and laid them out in the pattern of a maze on my lawn. When I returned from Crete I walked it almost every morning at dawn to get inspiration for my novel about Minoan Crete. My daughter walked it most days when she returned home from school to calm her down after the day's events. It was in the shape of the first maze I describe in chapter 6 of *The Lily and the Bull*:

> At the time Ierii spoke her name before the queen, Quilla was in the sacred grove on the holy mountain. She had carefully laid out the pattern of a maze beneath the trees with small white stones. She had based her pattern on the sacred number seven and to walk it she passed the centre seven times before she reached it. The constant turning and bending of the path meant that at the end she had covered a great distance and yet had never moved farther than a few metres from where she had started.
>
> This type of maze had always been associated with the Goddess. It was inspired by the spiral, one of the most basic and evocative symbols in nature, and there was no question of getting lost within it. The path had no branches into which one was tempted. There was only one possible way to

go and that way led to the centre and out again. In the Cult of the Goddess it was used as a means to find the True Self. It was a way of slowing down from the busy rush of everyday life, of moving in an orderly progression, taking each step as one became ready for it, until the centre was reached which was at once the centre of the maze and the sensitive point of consciousness from which all Being springs.

From the stillness at the central point the pilgrim wound slowly outwards again to the exit which was, at the same time, the entrance. On reaching this he or she was ready to face whatever there was to face with a greater inner strength and calmness.

The Bull Cult had its own maze, but it was of the opposite type. It was deliberately designed to confuse and to foster fear. Within its cruel pattern one could wander helplessly, taking wrong turns down side alleys which led nowhere. It was a challenge in its own way and those who did not perish in it and found their way out emerged either aggressively elated and ready to command the world or crushed in spirit and ready to be commanded.

It was this second type of maze that was associated with Theseus and the Minator.

Three

Hebrides and Iceland in the Middle Ages

I: *The Weapons of the Wolfhound*

It is the twelfth century AD. Neil lives with his parents on a farm on the remote island of Lewis in the Outer Hebrides. He is bored with his days and longs for excitement. He makes friends with Brother Durston, a Christian hermit living in a rocky cell nearby. The hermit speaks to the boy about the virtues of forgiveness and peaceful coexistence, and teaches the value of contemplation and prayer.

But the visit of a Viking sea captain, Baldur, to the Island makes the boy restless. He goes with Baldur to Iceland to deliver a walrus ivory chess set carved by Brother Durston to Baldur's father — the Wolfhound. But Baldur's father has died, and his grave has been robbed of the hero's famous weapons. Baldur's anger is intense, and he and Neil go on a dangerous and exciting journey across Iceland to recover the stolen weapons — the Weapons of the Wolfhound.

The story deals with the contrast between the contemplative life and the life of violent adventure.

This book started for me when I saw a twelfth century chess set carved out of walrus ivory in the British Museum, and it was my first published book. I had been trying all my life to be a writer and only then, in my fiftieth year, did I succeed in getting anything but my poems published.

The chess pieces had been uncovered at Uig on the island of Lewis in the Outer Hebrides in the nineteenth century when a ploughman was ploughing a field. The tiny figures emerged as he turned over the soil. He ran terrified from the place, believing they were some devilish beings from the underworld. Later they were properly identified and ended up in the British Museum.

I stared at them for a long time pondering how such sophisticated pieces came to be in that field in such a place, so remote from the castles of Europe where such a game might be played. I didn't know at that time that the Vikings often played chess on their long journeys across the seas.

I began to visualise a monk who had lived in southern France at a great monastery and who became disillusioned with community life and retreated to a remote place to be a hermit. In the long winter months he would sit in his hut at Uig, storms howling outside, and carve the walrus ivory he found on the beach, dreaming of the great halls where he had hobnobbed with bishops and knights and kings and queens. The story grew.

My son Strat was at Oxford. I used to visit him at this time and sit in the magnificent round library of the Radcliffe Camera attached to the Bodleian Library, and do my research into the twelfth century — about which I knew very little. Those were very happy days. My years of child rearing were behind me and I was free at last to do something for myself. Learning about things had always given me great joy.

Rex Collings, a publisher of children's books, was interested in publishing the book, so I made my hero a fourteen year old boy who was torn between his friend the hermit, who represented the contemplative, mystical life of the spirit, and his friend the Viking sea captain with whom he ran away to Iceland, and who represented for me the dangerous, violent adventuring life of the body.

I had never been to either the Hebrides or Iceland at this time, though I had been to Scotland. I had of course seen photographs and films of both places, and imagination did the rest.

I only visited the Island of Lewis after the book was published when I was preparing to write a sequel, but I found I had been pretty accurate. For Iceland I drew not only on films, but on the recurring nightmare I had had since childhood about being in danger from erupting volcanoes. Many of the scenes were based on my childhood memories of the Drankensberg Mountains in KwaZulu-Natal Province, which had been extruded in a great sheet of molten lava in ancient time. I also drew on an experience at the summit of Mount Etna in Sicily where Oliver and Rachel and I were nearly asphyxiated by sulphurous fumes and only survived because the wind changed.

When Rex Collings agreed to publish *The Weapons of the Wolfhound* I asked a school friend of my son Julian, John Warricker, to design the cover. He has since become a well-known designer and artist.

II: *The Eye of Callanish*

Set at the beginning of the twelfth century AD on the island of Lewis in the Outer Hebrides, off the west coast of Scotland.

A young girl is persecuted for being in touch with the devil because she is fascinated by the Stones of Callanish, an ancient stone circle.

By January 1977 I was pronounced clear of angina by the doctor at Kings College Hospital. I told him about the miraculous healing I had had when I visited a spirit healer in Bristol — but he wrote down in his notes, "spontaneous remission". I wonder how many other doctors write that down when a patient has been to a healer and recovered. Surely if they don't believe it, they should still write down "she *believes* she was healed miraculously".

Rex Collings said he would be interested in a sequel to *The Weapons of the Wolfhound*, so I started thinking about a new story involving Neil and the hermit on the Isle of Lewis — but I was busy writing other books and did not complete it at that time.

In October 1977 I received a devastating letter from my sister Rhona, a born-again Christian and an enthusiastic member of a missionary organisation. She had read — or maybe only dipped into! — my "Tall Stones" trilogy, and accused me of doing the work of the devil. I was shattered and only pulled through because of the support of my friends and family who assured me my books did anything *but* the work of the devil. I received a letter from a reader that same week saying that my book was the only one she'd read that made "good" more interesting than "evil". Other letters poured in from readers all assuring me that the "Tall Stones" trilogy had saved them from despair and set them on a spiritual path.

I went for a short time back to the idea of a sequel for *The Weapons of the Wolfhound*, believing that, through the hermit, I could refute Rhona's accusations. I also later wrote an entire novel about a Christian saint, *Etheldreda*, in answer to that terrible letter.

But on the whole the sequel to *The Weapons of the Wolfhound* never took off at this time.

In September 1978 Oliver and I went to the Isle of Lewis for two weeks and I at last saw the landscape in real life that I had written about only from imagination in *The Weapons of the Wolfhound*.

We also visited Callanish, a magnificent group of standing stones on the other side of the island. This place had a powerful effect on me. Oliver spent the day drawing them and I wandered about touching them and reacting to them. I noticed an extraordinary black crystal in the silvery grey gneiss in the tallest and most imposing of the stones. If the stone had been a man the crystal would have been in the middle of his forehead in the position of the mythical third eye. I had the title for my new book: *The Eye of Callanish*. As we went about the island in those two weeks, I was living a second life in the twelfth century, with Neil, now older, and Mairi, and a white horse. The stones dominated my thoughts wherever we went.

But when I'd finished writing it back in London, Rex Collings was having financial problems and didn't want it after all.

Disappointed, I put it away in my cupboard and got on with the other books I was writing.

In April 1985 I seriously revised the book. I was reminded of my sister Rhona's horrible letter, because I read in the newspaper that a family in Wales, that very week, had been stoned because the villagers thought the mother was a witch. Her children had been persecuted at school and their lives made intolerable. It roused all my old anger at blind prejudice and bigoted fundamentalism fed by complacency and ignorance.

I returned to writing *The Eye of Callanish*, strengthening the theme that had only been hinted at before — the contrast between the true Christian, the hermit, and the false Christians who stoned the girl Mairi because she visited the Tall Stones of Callanish, which the medieval church had told them was the work of Satan.

The book was published in 1994 by Neue Erde in Germany,

but not in English until the e-book edition of 2001, and the Bladud Books edition in 2005.

The usual oddities happened to me during the writing of the book.

I was toying with the idea that the people who built Callanish had come over the seas from the west, when I met a yachtsman at a party who told me the idea was quite feasible because the currents flowing in that part of the Atlantic were more favourable to West to East sailing than in the other direction. I also read a Hopi legend by "coincidence" that was about two tablets of stone, inscribed by the Great Spirit, and given to two brothers. The one tablet was to be set up in the ancestral tribal lands and the tribe was to keep faithfully to the traditional ways. The other stone was to be taken by one of the brothers to the east. He was to travel in new lands and learn their ways. When he returned they should put the two stones together and at last the inscription would be understood. I loved this legend. Not only did it fit the theory that people had come from the west, but it seemed to me a profound statement that the ancient wisdom should not be pursued for its own sake (as many New Agers did) but that it should be put together with the new wisdom to illuminate both.

At the time I was working on the new version of *The Eye of Callanish*, my son Strat was on the east coast of North America. When he came back he brought me a beautiful chunk of pink granite (or gneiss) from the coast in NE America. I was amazed to see it matched exactly the pieces of rock I had brought back from the Isle of Lewis. I knew by the large crystals that they were both cooled deep in the earth and were probably very ancient igneous rocks. I learned very soon that they were exactly the same rock and, in fact, had been broken off from the same bedrock pulled apart millions of years ago by continental drift. I held the two pieces of rock in my two hands and fantasized that I was holding the two continents together again.

Four

Space Fiction

Child of the Dark Star

"There was a planet once called Earth. Its people, scattered like seeds before the wind, came to rest on Agaron..."
Astrologers have formed a rigid caste system on the new planet and is up to the hero to overturn it.

The impetus for writing *Child of the Dark Star* came from several sources. One was the hypnotic trance experience I had on 6 June 1978, which later became the first chapter of *The Son of the Sun*. The loneliness and suffering of the ancient Egyptian boy oracle I had experienced then, left me so disturbed that I knew I had to write about it in order to control my emotions about it, and yet I dreaded tuning in to that painful experience again. In February 1979 I decided to write a book set on another planet, in the future, incorporating the experience. As an added precaution I transferred the details to a girl living on this planet. I thought this would 'lay the ghost' for me. It did not.

I sometimes have dreams that teach me something significant, and if I write them down as soon as I wake I find I have important material to weave into the books I write.

These words were repeated to me twice clearly in a dream on the night of 10 January 1978. After the first hearing I woke and thought: "That is important. I must write it down." But I was sleepy and lazy and turned over and went to sleep again. When they were repeated I jerked awake and wrote them down exactly as they had been said in the dream. I later incorporated this passage into chapter 14 of *The Child of the Dark Star*:

Atman was given the secret of the universe as a gift.

He was pleased, but he did not know what to do with it. He did not know what it was, so he played with it as though it were a bauble or a toy. Eventually he hung it on a tree as decoration. That was what it was to him... decoration. Not for use.

So it was for a long time... until one day someone came who recognised it for what it was and bargained Atman for the unconsidered trifle.

Atman sold it to him for an artefact, and went off satisfied that he had struck a good bargain, rejoicing in his newly acquired artefact.

The one who now had the secret of the universe saw that it was a seed and planted it in his garden.

It grew to be the Tree of life and he sat in its shade in the heat of the day filled with great reverence and love.

All things were clear to him.

All things were good.

Meanwhile Atman began to grow dissatisfied and miserable.

The artefact no longer pleased him. He was bored with it. He had done whatever there was to be done with it on the first day and thereafter he could find out nothing new about it.

The man who had the secret of the universe however was never bored... its variation was infinite... his interest in it ever deepening.

At last Atman, having realised his mistake came to the man and asked for it back.

But now the price of it was so high Atman could not pay it.

He went away and worked for endless aeons to earn the

price of the thing he had sold so carelessly and so cheaply before.

"When I get it back", he thought, "I will never let it go, for indeed, it is the only thing worth having."

Among the themes in the plot of this novel I posit a group of 'sleepers', frozen beings from another planet who lie deep in caverns under the ground, but who control activity on the surface by telepathic dreaming. I was aware of an ancient Greek legend mentioned by Sextius Sylla in a work by Plutarch ("The Face of the Moon") where the Titan Cronos is defeated by Zeus and doomed to sleep forever. He is attended by servants who pass on his dreams as instructions to the world.

There are also many legends about heroes who sleep, ready to rise again when they are needed. For instance, the Seven Sleepers of Ephesus. I myself have experienced telepathic dream communication between family and friends. How much more of our dreams come from an outside source, we cannot tell.

When my friend Kirsten read the book she was very excited about this particular aspect of it. She had just been told an amazing story which her informant swore was true, about the American military finding several transparent sarcophagus-like boxes deep under ground, containing gigantic sleeping figures. They had done everything in their power to open them, but had failed. So they had reburied them in a top secret site until such time as they could figure out how to open them. I did not hear about this until after my book was published. This may be truth or it may be fantasy — but whatever it is it is at least part of one of the realms of our consciousness. I suppose I was also thinking of the possibility of cryogenics.

Another source of inspiration for *Child of the Dark Star* was my fascination with a pure rock crystal skull found in Mexico and displayed in the British Museum of Mankind in London. When I first encountered it I spent a long time gazing at it. Many strange thoughts came to me, and eerie dreams haunted me at night.

Not much was known about the skull at that time. It is almost impossible to date rock crystal carving. Since then doubt has been thrown on its antiquity, but for me, it will always have a powerful and disturbing, timeless, magic.

Almost 20 years after I first saw the skull and wrote it 'into' my novel, I read a book called *The Mystery of the Crystal Skulls* by Chris Morton and Ceri Louis Thomas (published by Thorsons, 1997). It seems there is a widespread Native American legend about the existence of thirteen crystal skulls which have lain hidden since ancient times, but which will be discovered one by one. When all are gathered together, a powerful prophetic force will be released and mankind will be given knowledge that will make sense of every mystery since the beginning of time.

Evidently versions of this legend may be found among the descendants of the Maya and the Aztecs of Central America, and many of the tribes of native Americans in North America. The version that particularly struck me as appropriate to my book is the Cherokee one, where it is said that each of twelve crystal skulls is assigned to an inhabited planet, with the thirteenth presiding in some way over them all.

In my novel the crystal skull is part of a malevolent force on a distant inhabited planet. The Morton and Thomas book does not describe the skulls as malevolent, but then Knowledge received before time by people who are not ready for it has often triggered the release of a dangerous and destructive energy.

Another trigger incident for *Child of the Dark Star* was a remark reported to me by a friend, Michael, who met a woman who attracted him on a coach in Greece. He spoke to her and they were getting on well until she asked him what 'star sign' he was. When he told her she insisted on moving away, because, she said, their signs were not compatible. Later, she must have thought better of it, because they got married.

This led to my inventing a society on which astrologers had imposed a rigid caste system. The hero, who should have been killed at birth because, under his star, he would be expected to be a psychopath or criminal, survived, and worked to overthrow the injustice of the system.

When it was first written it was accepted at once for publication by Corgi. They typeset it and sent me the proofs to correct of both text and colourful cover.

And then I received a letter to say they had decided to drop it. I had to wait until 1984 for it to be published again. I hated the new cover.

In 2001 it was published as an e-book and in 2005 in paperback with a cover I like: the crystal skull with the stars of the Universe gleaming through it.

Five

Dark Ages Britain

The Tower and the Emerald

Viviane, a beautiful Celtic princess, unwittingly unravels the spell that binds the spirit of the evil Idoc within a circle of tall stones. Once released, the sorcerer-priest uses his powers to deliver vengeance upon those responsible for his original enslavement — including the Princess Viviane.

From 14–21 July 1979 Oliver and I stayed at a cottage in Monyash with Shirley Toulson and a couple of her friends. Shirley was writing a book on the ancient trackways of the Derbyshire area and Oliver was to do the illustrations for it. It was called *Derbyshire: Exploring the Ancient Tracks* and was first published by Wildwood House in 1980.

One of the places the author wanted illustrated was the recumbent circle of huge stones at Arbor Low. We reached it by walking through a dirty and depressing farmyard. The animals looked unhealthy and neglected, and the atmosphere was dark and unpleasant.

The stone circle was the first I'd seen with all the stones lying down like a gigantic clock face. Oliver went off at once to draw a neighbouring tumulus, while I stayed in the circle. Usually I feel happy in stone circles — with the possible exception of Rollright in Oxfordshire where I sensed 'black magic'. At Arbor Low I felt depressed and uneasy and began to feel that someone was buried at the centre, though there was no physical indication that this was so and, indeed, it is very rare, though not unknown, for there to be a burial in a stone circle. I sat on the henge surrounding it and puzzled about it.

As I did so I began to feel very strange. I was now convinced that there was a man buried — not only buried but somehow imprisoned there. There was a terrible feeling of darkness and evil. I seemed to hear a voice in my head pleading to be released.

'How?' I asked.

And then it seemed to me he was telling me to walk a spiral to the centre, and then unwind the spiral as I walked out again.

Trance-like, I began to do this. Suddenly I experienced a kind of demonic joy, and stopped short. What was I doing? Why was the man's soul trapped there? Was he the source of the darkness and evil I felt all around me? If so, how could I release this on the world?

Perhaps his soul had been pinned to this place for good reason. I was aware of the man urging me time and again to continue, pleading that he was innocent and that he had been the victim of injustice perpetrated by evil and corrupt priests. He almost convinced me and I took a few more steps. But then I stopped again. How could I be sure? I was in an agony of indecision. Suddenly I pulled myself together and ran out of the circle — straight out, with no spiral path. I went at once to Oliver and told him the story. He continued drawing, but listened as he always did — making me feel 'earthed' and safe again.

That night, and every night we were in that cottage, I had the same terrible dream. In the dream I was one of five priests who were performing a ritual at the stone circle. At the centre was a man. We had broken both his legs so that he could not leave the spot. We circled him, chanting a spell. At one point I made the mistake of meeting his eye. He was staring right into mine and winked at me as though he was marking me in some way. I felt he knew I would never be free of him and that I would eventually release him. I was terrified, knowing that he was immensely evil.

The wink was sinister and menacing, indicating collusion.

We killed him by throwing five spears into him and continued the circling and the chanting, weaving a spell that he would stay there forever. He would never travel to the many realms of being beyond this one. No future generations would be harmed by his reincarnated body. I hadn't noticed at first that there were thongs tied to the standing stones, nor that the soil around the stones had been dug and loosened, but after we had finished the ritual the stones were pulled down by hundreds of people outside the circle. The chanting of the priests, the drumming of the drummers, all contributed to the power of the force that eventually toppled the stones. The circle was to hold the man forever. It would never be used for religious rituals again.

This dream, vivid in every detail, repeated itself every night of that week.

I had determined not to go back to the circle, but I realised I would never be free of the dream until I did something about it.

I believed now that the man was evil, but I also believed that no one should deny another the right and opportunity to change and develop through the many realms of being beyond this one. I had always hated the idea of excommunication in the Roman Catholic Church.

On the last day we were in the district I went back to the circle and I walked the spiral to the centre. I stood there and said a fervent prayer to The Christ and the Angel Gabriel that this man's soul should be released under their control and into their care. And then I unravelled the spiral. As I reached the outer rim I noticed that the black clouds that had been lowering over the district all day had lifted and buttercups were blazing golden in the sunlight. It was almost as though bubbles of light were rising from the circle and floating away into the sky. I felt a tremendous release and joy. I have never had the dream again. But the story is not quite over.

Weeks later Shirley discovered during her research that the body of a man had in fact been found buried at the centre of the stone circle at Arbor Low and that his lower leg bones were missing, as though they had been amputated at the knee. In her book she says: 'Was this done as an urgent practical measure to prevent the sacrificial victim making a final bid for freedom, or was it a partly magical, partly symbolic, gesture to stop his spirit walking the hills?' (*Derbyshire: Exploring the Ancient Tracks*). It was during the excavations of Harold St George Gray that the skeleton of the man had been found. The date of his burial is not known.

On 8 November 1980, Oliver and I were guests at a dinner party at the house of some people in Beckenham we had only just met. Arbor Low came into the conversation and I launched into the story of what had happened to me there. Suddenly all the candles on the table blew out and the man sitting next to me fell back in his chair. Oliver and I looked at each other in horror and very soon made our excuse to leave.

I wondered if the man who had fallen was perhaps one of the five priests in the original ritual, shocked at the ancient memory being revived.

From 9–16 December 1985 I was visiting a friend, Mikki, in Boston, USA. Again I told the story. Her other visitor, a young man, suddenly went very pale, and stood up as though to leave the table. But before he could do so he lurched forward, almost fainting. Was he another of the five?

In December 1983 my editor at Arrow asked me to write a fantasy novel to follow the "Guardians of The Tall Stones" trilogy. I suggested writing a novel about the mysterious black knight who appears so often to challenge the hero in the Arthurian stories, but the editor talked me out of it (although I managed to sneak him in as a minor character).

Because the experience at Arbor Low had been so disturbing and powerful I decided to set my new book around it. I called the new novel *The Tower and the Emerald*, bringing in the emerald that in legend had fallen from the crown of Lucifer, the great archangel, when he fell disgraced from heaven.

In my book a Celtic princess comes upon the circle with all the stones recumbent and, like me, encounters the imprisoned soul of a man. She releases him — but without the prayer I made. Together in a former life, they are now together again. He had not grown and changed through many lifetimes as she has, and the storyline of the book follows the often horrifying progress of their entanglement, until his eventual redemption.

In 1983, *The Secret Tradition of Arthurian Legend* by Gareth Knight was published. (Aquarian Press). I did not buy it or read it until much later, after my own book had been published, but when I did I read the following passage:

The flow of time referred to in the last paragraph might perhaps be represented by some of the spiral and maze patterns found on megalithic sites at Newgrange and elsewhere.

There are, as the report says, many such sites, some in a more effective state of operation than others. Certainly the author is aware that two Anglican clergy with particular psychic gifts and a specialized sense of vocation have been made aware of 'guardians' bound to old sites in the West of England. They had been bound there by magical means and remained there as captive souls until released, by the appropriate sacraments, from their centuries of spiritual bondage. They were apparently not priest kings but lesser mortals, victims of human sacrifice, probably in a later, degenerate phase of the system.

Much later than the incident itself, and indeed later than I wrote *The Son of the Sun* (1981–82) I learned that the ancient Egyptians were capable of imprisoning a soul by magic if they believed it was necessary. In *The Son of the Sun* it seemed to me that this is what had happened to Akhenaten.

I found out more about the sinister wink too. I remembered it with such dread from my recurring dream that I puzzled why, what was normally such a light-hearted gesture, should seem so threatening. Then someone told me that in the party game *Murder*, the murderer marks the intended victim with a wink. As so many children's games are based on ancient race memories of rituals, I wondered if this was such a case. And then, only this year, I shivered to read in *The Ancient Egyptian Pyramid Texts* (translated by R.O. Faulkner):

"O you who are winked at, beware of him to whom command has been given;
"O you to whom command has been given, beware of him who was winked at."

As is usual when I write a book based on a strange experience, other strange experiences tend to happen. In 1985, *The Tower and the Emerald* was published by Century Hutchinson and then by Arrow. In it I describe how the man released takes over the body of the Celtic princess's lover in order to lie with her again. I was working on this part of the book in April 1984 when a friend asked me to meet and talk to a Swedish friend of hers. 'Because,' she said, 'she is very worried by a strange thing that has been happening to her and you are the only one I know who might be able to offer her an explanation.'

It turned out the woman believed a lover from a former lifetime, a Japanese man, had taken over the body of her current lover. Sometimes he seemed possessed and made love to her in a totally different way from before. During those times he muttered things in Japanese though it was a language he did not know. She had consulted a medium and been told it was a case of possession.

That one should ever hear of such a case is extraordinary enough, but that I should hear of it in my own circle of friends, just when I was writing about it, was surely an extraordinary 'coincidence'.

As with all my novels, the story of *The Tower and the Emerald* is woven from different threads. The book may have started from that extraordinary and disturbing experience at Arbor Low, but many perennial themes from myth and legend are woven into the story to illuminate certain facets of the human condition.

A strong theme throughout the book is the conflict of interest between Nature (the Green Lady, the Earth Goddess) and the dark destructive forces wielded by the human race in pursuit of immediate material gratification. Lucifer's emerald plays an important symbolic role as the lost balance between matter and spirit.

At the time I was writing the book I was spending a great deal of time studying the Kabbalah, mainly through the easy-to-read books by Z'ev ben Shimon Halevi (Warren Kenton) for example, *A Kabbalistic Universe* (Rider, 1977) and *The Way of the Kabbalah* (Rider, 1976), and *A Practical Guide to Kabbalistic Symbolism* by Gareth Knight (Helios Book Service, 1965). I became fascinated by the Sephirotic Tree of Life — the mighty scheme of things. In *The Tower and the Emerald* (chapter 1) I wrote:

> She chose an oak, the tallest she had ever seen, standing like a
> giant, its girth such that two tall men with long arms
> stretched to the limits would find difficult to encompass. It
> rose straight and true, branches balanced and harmonious, its

crown almost out of sight. She circled it several times, and then touched it... She began to feel something of the tremendous forces which coursed through it, which drove it up towards the sky. She put her hands on the bark and felt through her own flesh that upsurge of energy. Totally silent and with no sign of movement, the tree yet was vibrant with action. Beneath her hand prodigious events were taking place, so minute that they could not be seen with the eye, yet so powerful that the mighty Being of the tree was continually being created and renewed... its roots driving deep in the earth with the strength to crack rock and tumble mountains.

[...]

Whether it was the extraordinary concentration of sunlight that made the tree seem to vibrate and change before her very eyes, or whether there was a kind of magic in the air channelled through Brendan, she could not be sure... but the natural living tree before her began to take on a visionary quality. It became for her the mysterious Tree of Life, reaching up through all the Realms of Being to the very borders of that region where not even the archangels dare penetrate...

She realised that the Tree was growing as much downwards from above, as though rooted in the Light of Heaven, as it was growing upwards from below, where it was rooted in the World of Changes, the World of Matter.

She saw herself as Spirit from the highest realms, rooted now in the earth, but striving to return. She saw around her the world of air, earth, fire and water: the multitudinous beings of the World of Matter. And above her she saw the non-material World of the Soul, the region of angels and of demons, of elementals and of those who are awaiting rebirth. She knew that beyond this there were other realms, still out of reach of her understanding even in her most inspired moments: the Realm of pure Spirit where the mighty archangels observe and act — known to pagans as 'the gods' — even they still far from the threshold of the Unknown, the Dwelling of the Nameless One.

Viviane felt her head burning with the struggle to understand all that was coming to her.

She envisaged the Tree with energy flowing up and down from the First to the Last, the One to the Many, and back again. She saw spheres and realms contained within the Tree, each with its precise meaning and function. She saw beings going up and down and up again, animated by the tremendous lightning flash' of God's desire for life, yet freely motivated by their own longing to explore before their yearning to rejoin their source drove them back, transformed and enriched.

She saw those who rose and those who fell. She saw those who tried and tried again, and those embittered and failed beings who had given up trying…

A passage that arose purely and simply from a telepathic experience can be found in Chapter 6 of the Century edition, but I left it out at the Mushroom eBook and Bladud Books paperback editions because I later felt it was irrelevant to the story.

Resolutely Viviane entered the fissure and worked her way along it. She began to feel, and then to hear, a strange throbbing — as though she was in touch with the giant heart of the very earth itself. Then she noticed a light faintly flickering at the far end of the tunnel. She extinguished her own torch and crept forward as quietly as possible, hoping to see without being seen. The throbbing soon became deafening. As her own voice had grown and changed and multiplied into many voices, so every sound was distorted and magnified. Viviane negotiated a difficult bend in the passage, inching her way round a rock that was delicately balanced on another, and she was suddenly confronted by a terrifying and extraordinary scene.

She stood on a ledge high above the floor of a gigantic cavern, looking down on thousands of naked bodies, shining with oil and sweat in the wavering light of hundreds of torches. The throbbing came from the drums being beaten, and from the stamping of thousands of bare feet on the dusty floor. The stamping churned up the dust and it filled the place with an angry red haze.

On the night of 1 February 1984 I had written this passage under a strange compulsion. I did not think it out or even consider whether it was relevant to the book or not. I 'experienced' it.

Early next morning my daughter Rachel phoned from Rome

very shaken, saying that she had had a horrid experience the night before. She had been taken to a pop concert in Rome. When they arrived they found they had to push their way through a very narrow crowded passage where she felt like fainting from the pressure around her. When eventually they came out of the passage they found themselves upstairs looking down on a huge crowd below. As the concert got going the people downstairs held up candles and lighters, stomping and waving them to the music. "'Like a lot of savages," she said. I counted it as a case of telepathy.

A passage in chapter 3 of *The Tower and the Emerald* was written as a direct result of a visit to Bayham Abbey on 15 July 1981. The abbey is in Sussex, between Lamberhurst and Tonbridge Wells. I was tremendously excited by a gigantic tree growing behind the ruined altar, its roots inextricably woven into the stone:

> At the eastern end she found a table of stone, the huge slab cracked across but not yet fallen. Behind it the ruined walls formed a semicircle, and from them grew a huge beech tree, its silver-grey branches spreading wide, shimmering with light. Awed, she stood and gazed up at it, drinking in its force and beauty, its energy, its power.
>
> She put out a hand to touch what she thought was a low-lying branch but found that it was a root, the blocks of the ancient wall and the roots of the tree so intertwined that it was impossible to decide whether the building was turning into a tree, or the tree into a building.

I based Idoc's dark scrying mirror of polished obsidian on the scrying mirror of John Dee in the British Museum. John Dee was an Elizabethan genius whose scientific work on navigational systems gave the seafaring expeditions of his contemporary countrymen a huge advantage over other countries, yet who died vilified for his interest in magic, the windows of his elegant London house stoned by angry mobs.

The little creatures I invented called 'voyeurs' are directly based on my hatred of the intrusive nature of the media (witness, the death of Diana, Princess of Wales) and indeed our own sometimes overweening curiosity about our neighbours and celebrities.

The Tower and the Emerald (chapter 10):

It was possible they had witnessed the destruction of the mirror. They seemed to appear everywhere — perching, prowling, watching everything that went on; relentless sight-seekers, sniffing out trouble and rushing to where it was to pry and peep; slobbering greedily over sexual couplings and gloating over suffering. He had even been half aware of them during the battle, shrilling to each other excitedly to come and see some young man horribly dismembered, clucking their teeth in hypocritical disapproval even as their eyes swelled larger and larger with excitement.

    He strode to the door and flung it open again. The macabre little sight-seekers, the voyeurs, were still crowded there, their bowl-shaped ears pressed to the wood, fighting over which should get its eyeball to the keyhole. When Idoc appeared they immediately fell back in terror, but he managed to seize one by its thin, bird-bone leg. Its mates shrieked with excitement as he dragged it into the chamber, then they surged forward again, obviously feeling no sympathy for the victim, only delight that they would have yet another drama to enjoy.

    The voyeur itself was not so happy about being forced to take a central part in the action for once. It squealed and bit and scratched its oppressor, the weasel teeth and small filthy talons uncomfortably sharp. Idoc held the creature at arm's length and shook it violently until it hung from his hand like a dirty rag. Its whole being seemed to shrivel with despair. Even the bulbous eyes, which had been such a feature of its face, retreated into the skull, leaving only two heavily lidded slits, through which Idoc could catch the glint of a venomous stare.

In Chapter 9, the silver fish that yielded such a powerful spiritual charge to Viviane is based on an experience of my own with a little silver fish I bought at Glastonbury in 1975. I had sat up all one night writing poems about Christ expressed through the symbol of the Fish. It was one of the most profound experiences of my life.

Many are the references to crystals in the story, most of them based on crystals in my own possession which I have imbued with magical properties for the purpose of the story. I was once given a rough chunk of rose quartz and a geologist friend cut and shaped it into a crystal ball for me. I had had it in my possession for some time before I noticed that turned to the light in one specific way a star seemed to shine out from just above the surface like a hologram.

The Tower and the Emerald (chapter 13):

> Inside she found an exquisite sphere of crystal, shining softly with light the colour of pink rose petals. She gazed into its depths. She turned it from side to side. She trembled at its beauty. Suddenly she thought she saw a star in its depths; but as soon as she held it still the star vanished. She turned it round again. Nothing. And then, suddenly, it was there! It seemed to hover above the surface, yet when she tried to touch it, to pick it off, she found it was deep inside the crystal ball, an ephemeral shadow of light, lighter than light... the spirit of light... there and not there...

Another of my own crystals I used in the story was a double-ended quartz crystal. That it was perfectly six faceted at each end fascinated me. It was complete. Usually the quartz crystals I saw had been ripped off a matrix and only one end was faceted.

The Tower and the Emerald (chapter 6):

> Wonderingly she picked it up and held the two points between her thumb and index finger. She could feel the power of it surging through her hand and almost dropped it. But the beauty of it held her riveted. Light reflected off all the crystal planes, and yet it was as clear as air. Through it she could see the trees...the slope of the hill...the clouds... images of the natural world reflected back and forth within the crystal, from plane to plane. She turned the crystal around and around, watching the light change...the reflections running into each other, becoming blurred and indistinct until, emerging from them, she saw new images... figures and forms of light... silver beings as insubstantial as gossamer yet having the strength to move mountains and fell giants... A thousand angels on a needle point — each

one capable of overthrowing an emperor or of making a peasant into a king.

In chapter 8, I refer to an amethyst crystal that I also have in my possession. In the story it is capable of dispelling illusion, and that seems not too far from the truth. To me the power of crystals lies in their astonishing transparent beauty and the fact that they remind me that I am on a planet hurtling through a magnificent universe. Experiencing that alone should make one see things in a different way and reject the illusions that surround one in everyday life.

On 17 May 2001 I watched a television programme on Channel 4 in the series "Secrets of the Dead: Murder at Stonehenge". It was about the discovery of a decapitated body in a shallow grave at Stonehenge. Research revealed that it was buried in Saxon times in the seventh Century AD. The implication was that it was a man punished for a crime so bad that he was buried by Christians at a pagan site so that his soul would be damned and never make it to heaven. At that time the tension between Christians and pagans was very intense.

It suddenly occurred to me that this might have been the reason for the burial at Arbor Low as well.

The body at Arbor Low has never been dated. I assumed the incident had occurred in ancient times, although I was puzzled, knowing that stone circles were not used for burials in Neolithic times.

This raises an interesting point about knowledge gained by psychic means. One may "pick up" something of a transmission, but there may be interference or "static", and one only receives part of a memory or message. Like when we hear a few words across a crowded room, we fill in the rest of the conversation by guesswork, and, probably more often than not, get it wrong.

I might have picked up psychically that someone was buried at the centre of the circle at Arbor Low, and that he was buried there to prevent his soul progressing to the other world, but I might have got the timing wrong. It might well have been an early Christian punishment of the type described in the Stonehenge programme.

The immediate message I received from the experience I had

at Arbor Low may have been only that: 'Change is written into the constitution of the Universe, and if one denies a person the right to change we are denying him a fundamental right.' But during the writing of the book, much more came to me that I hadn't recognised at the time. It was implicit, and spreading out exponentially from the original intent.

Six

Eighteenth Dynasty Egypt

Akhenaten: Son of the Sun
Hatshepsut: Daughter of Amun
Tutankhamun and the Daughter of Ra
The Ghost of Akhenaten

I: *Akhenaten: Son of the Sun*

The narrator of this story, set in Eighteenth Dynasty Egypt, is fictional, but he is a protagonist in, and observer of, historical events. c.1353–1335 BC.

The Temples at this time used child oracles, and this boy is one such, taken away from his parents at birth and kept in the Temple as a virtual prisoner, to speak to the gods. When he is rebellious he is punished. But for him (as for any ancient Egyptian) the thing that worried him the most was that he was never given a name. Without a name, the Egyptians believed, you could have no proper existence.

During the unfolding of the story he is befriended by Prince Amenhotep, who later becomes the Pharaoh Akhenaten, given a name, and taken out of the dark oppressive Temple of the God Amun. He becomes a close colleague and confidant when Akhenaten overthrows the powerful priests of Amun and raises to power his favourite god, the Aten.

He is there in the good and golden years when Akhenaten and Nefertiti are riding high, idealistically founding a new royal city and a new religion.

He is there when it all turns sour, Akhenaten becomes a tyrant and is assassinated, and Nefertiti dabbles in forbidden black magic.

The inspiration for this book came to me following a series of bizarre experiences and disturbing events, which continued during and after the writing of the book. I am not sure the story behind the story is finished yet.

On 6 June 1978 two friends and I tried a form of mild hypnosis that was supposed to give us recall of past lives, described in *Windows of the Mind* and *World's Within* by G.M. Glaskin, published by Wildwood House, 1974 and 1976.

Because I had always thought I might have had a life at the time of Hatshepsut, a female pharaoh of the Eighteenth Dynasty, I decided I would try deliberately to take myself back to her time to research a book I was preparing to write about her. I lay relaxed, one friend massaging my ankles, one my forehead.

Before going under I thought hard about everything I knew about Hatshepsut and her times, and when I began to see pictures they were indeed of a female in ancient Egypt who could well have been Hatshepsut. My friends asked me questions and I replied from my relaxed, half trance-like state. But a niggling doubt began to trouble me. I did not feel as though the experiences were real.

I had decided I would terminate the session when suddenly I felt as though I had been hit in the chest and something seemed to explode in my head. When the shock subsided I found myself still in ancient Egypt, but caught up in a totally different experience. This experience is what I have now faithfully described in the first chapter of *Akhenaten: Son of the Sun*.

My friends listened fascinated, aware that the quality of this experience was very different from the last. They kept asking me my name, and I kept screaming that I had no name.

'What do they call you?' my friends persisted.

'They call me by the names of those who speak through me,' I cried. 'They say that they are the gods, but they are not the gods!'

I was experiencing the loneliness, the fear, the despair of a young boy who was kept prisoner by a corrupt priesthood and brought out only for ceremonies when he was to speak as oracle.

I had at that time not realised how vitally important the Name was to the ancient Egyptians: so important that if a criminal was to receive the worst punishment possible, his name was removed from him. Without a name he fell back into the Void at death and ceased to be. My friends were amazed how terrified I was that I had no name.

What I was experiencing so vividly at the moment I picked up the boy's memory was the horror of being sealed in a chamber at the centre of a pyramid. All my senses were responding to the situation — even to smelling the resin as the door was sealed.

Eventually I jerked out of my trance shrieking that I *would not* return to my body. I found myself weeping and feeling ill in my present incarnation in my sitting room in London. My friends said I should write a book about the boy oracle and forget about Hatshepsut. But I couldn't bear to contemplate it. It seemed to me that the boy must have died in that chamber in the pyramid and I had 'picked up' the experience of it millennia later. Was it a case of 'possession' or of 'far memory'? Either way I did not want to go through those emotions again.

In 1979 I wrote *Child of the Dark Star*, set in the future on another planet, and used the idea of a child oracle imprisoned and exploited by a corrupt priesthood. I hoped this would satisfy the need I felt to tell the story I had experienced under hypnosis that day, without going through the emotional trauma that had accompanied it.

But of course the story would not leave me alone.

Various things continued to happen which made me more and more convinced I had a real connection with that nameless oracle in Egypt. Time and again clairvoyants had told me that I was a medium and yet I shied violently away from the suggestion, determined never to allow anyone, alive or dead, to manipulate my mind 'again'. I began to notice that I always used the word 'again', and this even before the hypnosis experience.

For some time a friend, T, who is an astrologer, medium and healer, had been asking if I would let her 'take me back' into past lives. My usual caution caused me to refuse. It is one thing to accept insights that come personally and directly when one can use one's own mechanism for testing truth and falsehood, and another to accept an outsider's vision and opinion.

She was so persistent that at last, on 4 February 1982, I gave in and agreed.

I arrived at T's apartment in Chelsea at 5 pm. She lit candles and we prepared to relax and to "drift through Time".

Under her guidance I let my mind drift until pictures began to form. She questioned me and I told her what I saw. On more than one occasion she interrupted and described to me exactly what I was 'seeing' seconds before I told her about it.

> I was being carried on a flat bier — a young man of about eighteen — bare chest, short white pleated kilt with broad gold belt extending in front the length of the kilt. Head covered by something that could have been a crown. Arms

crossed on breast. I was carried on the shoulders of muscular, dark skinned men. Above me arched a very high, blue sky with two hawks circling slowly.

Sleepily I watched the hawks watching me — listened to the scuffle of feet on the dusty ground, the creak of the wooden bier, the fluttering of black ostrich feathers at the corners of the bier. There were crowds lining the route. I could hear them talking in the distance, but as soon as the bier approached, there was absolute silence, and everyone bowed.

I was carried into a temple — into a dark, gloomy hall, the only light from braziers, flickering long shadows. Tall columns disappearing into the gloom above. I shivered with the sudden chill and felt a twinge of distaste and fear.

I was placed before a statue of Anubis, the god of death, and rose from the bier. I could hear chanting but did not take much notice of it. Two priests led me round the back of the statue to a hidden chamber. There I sat on a gilded, winged chair, back straight, staring ahead. I was aware I had been moving like an automaton, my mind slow and sluggish.

I had the feeling that the priests would gladly have done away with me if they could — but they dared not. I was clairvoyant and they were not. The people demanded and expected prophecies and guidance from the spirit world which, in the old days, the priest-kings had provided. Now they were not capable of it. Misuse of their power and the appointment of the wrong men for the wrong reasons had lost them the skill and the right to speak directly with the gods.

From the darkness that surrounded me there emerged horrible demonic shapes, half animal, half man. They circled me snarling and snapping, reaching for me, but never quite coming out of the shadows.

'You can no longer frighten me,' I thought. 'You are thought-forms conjured by the priests all these years to rule me by fear. But I no longer fear you. I know you for what you are!'

The vision faded. T in London 1982 AD, asked me to try to see some years ahead.

I saw a man clad as a pharaoh, a beautiful woman beside him. All around us buildings were being constructed. I could hear the noise — smell the dust. There was a feeling of excitement and elation. These temples would be full of light and air — very different from the old ones which had been so dark and secretive.

I pulled myself out of the vision now, somewhat shaken.

T was convinced I had seen Akhenaten. That, indeed, I *was* Akhenaten.

But I knew that I was not.

She herself then went into deep trance and spoke with a man's voice claiming to be 'Horus'. 'He' said it was my duty to use the knowledge I was being given. He said I must try to recall everything about this past life. Writing this book would be my greatest work. My other books had just been preparation for this. He suggested I lay awake thinking about it before I went to sleep each night, and then write down what came to me as soon as I woke.

As I left my friend's house I was awed, confused, scared. I did not know what to believe. It would all have seemed like sheer craziness to me if there had not been so many things in my life that had led me to believe that such things were possible.

Pharaoh Akhenaten has always been, and still is, a mystery to all those who look at the long history of ancient Egypt. What drove him to break with several millennia of settled and powerful tradition to establish so bravely a new and revolutionary religion? To what extent did he succeed in introducing monotheism into a polytheistic society? To what extent did he fail? Those who came after him called him 'criminal' and 'heretic' and tried to remove all trace of him from history. For many centuries he was forgotten. The King Lists at Abydos do not mention him. Why has he now become the most popular and interesting of pharaohs? Why are so many books written about him? Why are so many museums guarding the few remnants of his extraordinary life so jealously?

I had never intended to write a book about Akhenaten, but I began to write *The Son of the Sun* nevertheless.

In the first chapter of *The Son of the Sun* I described the experience I had had under hypnosis on 6 June 1976.

As I wrote, all sorts of strange things kept happening. Information began to pour in on me from directions I least expected. I did a great deal of academic research, but dreams, books opening at random, strangers met on buses, trains or at parties, gave me information I needed just when I needed it.

One dream in particular disturbed me:

I was beside a pool with a crowd of people who seemed excited about something. It seemed they had been working on a project for some years and were now testing it. I realised they were scientists and occultists. Strange partners! They had two tiny dried objects like small beetles and set them into a toy boat upon the pool. I peered closer and saw the two were minute people, one an ancient Egyptian princess, the other her servant. As they floated on the water they seemed very excited and happy.

But then the boat overturned, and the servant was drowned.

I was given the princess to look after. I held her close to my face and spoke very softly to her. She told me there was an afterlife and we did see again the people we had loved. As I walked with her I nearly stumbled over obstacles. Somehow I was guided over them — though I did not see who helped me.

I remember I wanted to keep her safe and out of reach of the crowds who followed us. Someone drew near her and boomed out in a loud voice. She began fluttering and trying to escape from the huge faces pressing in around her and the terrible sound of their loud voices. I began to look around for something to put her in to keep her safe and found a glass jar, but as I lowered her into it, still frantically struggling, she damaged herself against the sides and before I could get the lid on she made a great effort to climb out and was squashed as the lid came down.

I was horrified. I had destroyed someone who had been alive 3000 years and had been placed in my care. I had put an end to something that had taken the scientists and occultists of the world, working together, millennia to achieve.

At that point I woke up.

I lay awake and worried about the book I was writing. I was 'bringing to life' people who had lived 3000 years ago. It was a great responsibility. Would I in fact destroy them in the process?

T told me I had a guide in the Spirit World and I must listen to him.

"What is his name?" she asked me.

And, without thinking, I replied: "Khurahtaten". Only afterwards I realised "Khu" means shining spirit, "Ra", the Sun God, and "Aten" the divine sun disk worshipped by Akhenaten.

Information began to pour in on me from all directions. Like a magnet drawing iron filings to it, I found that once you are in a mood of high spiritual endeavour, relevant knowledge and experiences come to you.

On 15 March 1982 I found myself writing the following as though it were being dictated to me.

> The sculptor or embalmer makes the vessel and then, in the ceremony of 'opening the mouth' the statue or mummy is 'brought alive'; the door is opened, as it were, to let the spirit in to inhabit the house which has been prepared for it. The 'Ka' may then go in or out at will — not for its own sake, but for the sake of those left behind who need its help.
>
> There are many planes or realms beyond this earth one. The Ka comes from the one just beyond this one. Spirit guides and saints inhabit a higher one. But there are others we know nothing about.
>
> We should not be impatient to know what we are not ready to know. It is our duty to work to the best of our ability on the plane on which we find ourselves. We cannot hurry or slow our progress by willing it so. When we are in trouble we may ask for help from the next plane above, and those there who remember what it was like to live on the physical plane, may give us advice. But we must never take it without using our own intelligence to judge whether it is good or not.
>
> You have to 'open the mouth' of the dusty bones written about Egypt so that what was learned then can be learned now.
>
> Use stepping stones. You don't have to cross the river in one leap. That is what symbols, myths, legends, stories are — stepping stones from the familiar to the divine.
>
> Take something near — but further than you are now and try for it... stretch a little more... reach a little further.

Even so, after this encouragement, sometimes I would get angry and fling my pen down complaining that I did not want to write this book, that I didn't believe I had lived in Akhenaten's time and, even if I had, I couldn't remember enough to make a convincing book of it. Almost invariably T would phone me at this moment and say she had heard that I was having trouble. She even seemed to know the dreams I had been having!

But the inspiration for the book continued to come strong and strange. Words and visions came to me in dreams. When I ignored them they would recur until I was forced to take notice. If I was straying from what was supposed to be written I would suddenly fall asleep. I would literally 'pass out' for a few moments and 'come back' knowing that what I had just written was wrong. I would cross it out and try again. The words would flow and I knew they were closer to the mark.

At one point I decided to stop writing because I felt I should not go on until I had actually been to Egypt. Within 24 hours I met a group of people who were planning a trip to Egypt at the end of the year. They discussed what money each would need and they decided it had to be £500. The next day I received exactly £500 for something I had written. I told them I would go with them.

I did not intend to write any more of the book until the trip in December. But again I could not stop writing. I finished the book three days before I left for Egypt and was told by 'Horus', channelled through T, that I was not to be afraid, that he would accompany me and make sure I was given confirmation of what I had written.

I was afraid. I knew I had to face something in Egypt that I dreaded and had dreaded for millennia. I wrote this poem, this prayer to Horus:

Let your wings be my wings
O Horus, the sun's companion.
Teach me the currents of the air...
the high spiral
of the sky's heart...
the breathless pause
as the earth holds still
for the god to speak.
Fear has held my feet to the ground.
Fear has weighed me down.
My eyes and ears are blind and deaf with dust.

*Immortal Bird
shake me free,
turn me loose in your splendour...
Under your protection
let me soar.
Let me see the sun before its rising.
Let me see the world
at the point of transformation.*

We set off on 4 December 1982 and returned to London on 20 December, a small group of five, only two of whom I had met before, and one of them only once. Most of the original party had fallen away. They knew I was writing a book set in Akhenaten's time, but I had told them nothing about my experiences under hypnosis, nor what had passed between me and 'Horus'.

We stayed in Cairo and one of our first trips was inevitably to the pyramids on the Giza plain. In the taxi Beverley and Joseph talked about bribing someone to let us stay in the Great Pyramid overnight. I was horrified. I knew the experience would be exactly what I needed to check my book, but I was sick with fear, remembering 'the last time' I had been there. I tried to talk them out of it and when this failed, claimed that I would not be staying with them. They slipped away and returned with the deal set up. We could not stay overnight, but would have a few hours after closing time. We started climbing the long dark ramp within the Great Pyramid, pushed and jostled by sweating, talkative tourists. It was a nightmare: the crowds, the heat, the fear, the physical strain. I wondered if I was about to have a recurrence of my angina. My chest began to ache and I was sure I was going to have a heart attack. I could not bear to go forward, but it was impossible, because of the crowds, to go back. All this — and my ancient dread of the place as well!

When we finally reached the chamber I crawled into a corner and crouched there with my head to the wall. I was determined to leave with the last of the tourists. My friends were kind but firm. They told me that I should stay and face whatever it was I had to face or I would never be free of it. They were right.

I stayed.

I learned later that at the exact time this was happening to me my sister, Joan, thousands of miles away in South Africa, had become anxious about me. She felt I had been left behind in one of the Egyptian tombs and had been locked in for the night. She 'saw' me alone and terrified.

Under Beverley's instruction we sounded the OM as we walked around the sarcophagus. I would have preferred to stay quiet and work through my trial silently — but he insisted on ritual and, as it turned out, it was no bad thing.

The ancient syllable, the sound of all creation going about its business, reverberated deeply and magnificently in the chamber, dark now except for our one flickering candle. Then Jeanine, the Sanskrit scholar, began to chant a Vedic hymn:

That is the Whole.
This is the Whole.
From that Whole has this Whole come forth.
Having taken the Whole from the Whole,
Verily the Whole remains.'

She seemed a frail little person with a quiet voice but when she sang now her voice was as powerful and as beautiful as an opera singer's. The chamber reverberated around me and I, within it, began to resonate to the same rhythm. I felt the fear and darkness lift off me and float up with the sounds... up through the rock slab of the ceiling... through the five sounding boxes above (the chambers that the archaeologists say are to take the weight and pressure of the rock)... and out into the universe. With them I went — having one of those indescribable moments, outside Time and Space, when you know things it is not ordinarily possible to know...

I came out of that chamber walking on air — unafraid — renewed — confirmed in my deepest beliefs. I had not known at the time what the Sanskrit words meant, but they seemed to have the right effect nevertheless. Perhaps there is some way we understand words solely by intuition or telepathy.

In August 1983, almost a year after my experience of sounding the OM in the King's chamber that day, I read *The Unending Quest: The Reminiscence of Sir Paul Dukes KBE* (Cassell & Co, 1950). In Chapter 4 he wrote that he had sounded the OM in the King's chamber, and his description exactly described my own experience:

The note never ceased, for the echo continued to reverberate from the end of one breath to the beginning of the next. Louder tones seemed to billow in waves through the hall like peeling musical thunder.

In comparing notes afterwards Joseph said he had seen a shining white Horus bird with a golden crown hovering over us. Beverley had seen a winged Being with the face of a man and the body in the shape of a luminous double helix (the DNA molecule? The Caduceus, the staff of Hermes?). Neither had known that this was the chamber in which I had originally met Horus-Khurahtaten who had promised to meet me there again. I had not seen him, but I had felt a Presence. Jeanine had not planned to sing the hymn. It had just come to her. It was a Vedic hymn and this was Egypt. 'All is the One of Which I Am.'

It is known that Napoleon was left alone in the King's chamber of the Great Pyramid on 12 August 1799. Afterwards he refused to speak about what had happened there and said that he never wanted the incident to be mentioned again. 'What's the use? You would never believe me,' were his last words on the subject to Count Las Cases on St. Helena.

When we returned to London and people asked how long I had been in Egypt I didn't know what to answer. They expected me to say two and a half weeks — but such a count of days was meaningless. The journey was on many levels and in many different times. On the 'surface' level it was more of an assault course than a holiday, but on the other deeper levels it was a most valuable and extraordinary experience. In every ancient temple we visited, we meditated, and there was not one that did not yield some treasure to us. At the Temple of Luxor Jeanine called us into her 'special place', the inner sanctum, the little chamber restored by Alexander the Great. I entered without looking at it. The others were already beginning to meditate. Words came to my mind as though they were being spoken through me:

> Great God, creator of all the universes and all the realms within all the universes, who sends Servants of Light throughout all Time and Space to do Thy Will, to help and to guide those who are struggling… Send us forth in Thy Light… without fear and without weakness…

The vision that came to me was of shining wings encircling us and protecting us.

When we 'came back' and compared notes Jeanine had seen the wings surrounding us. Joseph had seen a circle of light containing a bird. When I looked up at the walls of the sanctuary for the first time I saw that there was a carved frieze of wings surrounding us.

At the Temple of Horus at Edfu I was aware of the figure of Christ on the plinth where the statue of Horus had once stood. Above him hovered the Horus — the hawk from whose wing feathers streamers of light descended, enclosing us. I looked up at the hawk and as I stared at it, it transformed into a dove. Afterwards Joseph told me he had seen a scarab above us, streamers of light descending from it. The scarab is the symbol of transformation. When I returned to London I read in the book *Serpent in the Sky* by John Anthony West (published by Wildwood House, 1979):

> Like all other initiatic teaching, Egypt held that man's purpose on earth was the return to the source. There were recognized in Egypt two roads to this same goal. The one was the way of Osiris, who represented the cyclic nature of universal process. This was the way of successive reincarnations. The second road was the way of Horus, the direct path to resurrection that the individual might achieve within a single lifetime. It is the Horian way that is the basis of the Christian revelation...

Still later (30 March 1983) I read on *p*.259 of *King Jesus* by Robert Graves (published by Hutchinson):

> John the Baptist roared in ecstasy. 'Look up, Lord, for your Ka descends upon you in the form of a dove!' Jesus looked up. At that moment the sun surmounted the eastern crag and shone brilliantly down upon the water [...] The Ka is the Weird, or double, of a King, and at the coronation of an Egyptian pharaoh is pictured as descending upon him in the form of a hawk...

As the journey progressed we found that Joseph and I often 'linked' in a vision. The experience in the Temple of Edfu was not the first or last time I was reminded that at the heart of all true religious experience, no matter what symbols are used and names are given, lies a revelation from the same Source.

One night I lay awake worrying that I was becoming more and more convinced that a great spiritual Being, using the symbolic form of the Horus hawk, was literally with us and, as a Christian, I should not perhaps have believed this. In the morning, before I had said a word about my worry, Joseph said he had had an extraordinarily vivid vision in the night: the Horus hawk perched on the rim of a Christian chalice and drinking from it.

I wrote in my diary (8 December 1982):

Bird on Chalice...
wild falcon...
Spirit Bird.
Thunder of wings stilled
for this deep draught.
Claws on silver clenched...
Blood–wine slaking thirst.
Liquid Life...
the Word
that began the worlds.
Light lifts
the mighty Horus
to the sky
that after this
the Eyes that saw all
might See All...
the Heart that knew all
might Know All.

At Hatshepsut's temple at Deir el Bahri, both Beverley and I heard singing when there was no one there to sing.

At Abydos I smelled incense in the temple of Seti I when there was no incense burning.

When we reached Luxor the group hired donkeys to go over the mountain to the Valley of the Kings. Most tourists go comfortably by taxi on the tarmac road around the base of the mountain. Again I tried to resist, believing that I was too old for the donkey. However, we went, and it was one of the most wonderful (and worst!) adventures of my life. Again Horus had seen to it that I would travel to the Valley of the Kings as I would have done thousands of years ago and that I would experience what an ancient Egyptian would have experienced. High above us in an unbelievably deep blue sky the Horus hawk hovered over us.

I wrote in my diary (10 December 1982):

I climb these bare rocks—
the skeletal remains of Time
scorched clean by the sun,
picked by the vultures…
and on the summit
face a sky
so darkly blue,
so vast
my human heart stops beating
and the heart I use
is the earth's heart,
the breath I draw
is the sky's breath.
Beneath these mountains
lie the empty tombs of kings
and beside me on the rock
stand the pharaohs themselves
seeing what I,
as man,
can't see…
If I turn my head quickly
will I catch
the flash of a hawk's wing…
the breast of Isis…
Maat's numinous feather…?
All around me I can feel them
but when I turn
I see nothing but dry, bleached stone
and the hot sky pressing down…
Grant, God of a million names,
that this moment
will stay with me
and be my guide

*when the noisy town
hits me
with a cloud of flies...
Grant, God who is beyond all names,
that I will know you
in the crowd.*

We did not go to Amarna, Akhenaten's city, although I longed to do so, and for a while I thought Horus had failed me in this respect. But when we returned to London I met up with an archaeologist who had worked for a long time on the site at Amarna and could tell me things and show me slides of places I would never have seen if I had visited as a tourist. She had actually worked in Akhenaten's tomb, and walked in the silence of the great waddi before they started to build a tourist road. Also back in London, a friend gave me detailed photographs of Amarna from his own visit.

We ended our journey at Aswan and there I had two experiences that I will never forget. We boarded a boat in the small hours and drifted on the Nile until dawn.

I wrote (16 December 1982):

*Mast threaded to the stars
this boat
silently in silence
glides,
darkness with its last breath
chilling our cheeks.
Even Time
is still.
A voice singing
silently in silence,
an ancient hymn...
opens the heart
to let the first light in.
Suddenly, with joy,
the sky is on the move with birds
and from the islands of ourselves
we greet each other.
Fish leap
and the boatman shakes out the sail.*

*Now the sun draws us home
along the gold thread
of the river…
and all
is festival.*

The other was Sehel Island at the first cataract, the ancient limit of the civilised world. Beyond this the wilds of Nubia reached into darkest Africa. Here on the border huge boulders had been carved with prayers and invocations from the earliest pre-dynastic times to the present day.

I wrote (17 December 1982):

*Before the Unknown
is always an island
or a holy mountain…
a place for the heart
to say a prayer,
inscribe a stone
or tell a bead.
This granite place
is such.
Here a man
is as alert to danger
as a dog
eating at a lion's kill.
Water violence
buffets the rocks.
The landscape beyond the frontier,
crouching,
holds in its shadows
alien ways
and alien thoughts.
From the first man to the last
the cry of the heart is the same.
Our comfort is
that it is the heart that is heard…
not the words…*

I read my manuscript on my return to London and did not feel I had to change a thing.

Confirmation of what I had written came to me in many different ways over the next few years, while I tried to find a publisher for the book.

For instance it was only on 27 September 1984 that I read in a book I picked up in a second hand bookshop that, according to Cagliostro, who had studied the Egyptian Mysteries, the great pyramid was used for divination through a child medium, and that child oracles were common in the Eighteenth Dynasty. (*The Magic of Obelisks* by Peter Tompkins, pub. Harper & Row, 1981).

Soon after my return from Egypt I visited T to report on my experiences there. I now had no doubt that I was 'meant' to write the book that I had at first so bitterly tried to avoid. The work had been punctuated by sloughs of despair alternating with high excitement — the whole so stressful that I was glad to be shot of it.

My relationship with T had become strained. I felt resentful that she was trying to influence the writing of the book. I felt very strongly it was a matter between me and my own sources of inspiration, and although I was prepared to listen to advice I did not want to be manipulated by anyone, alive or dead. Perhaps I felt so strongly because of my experience of being manipulated in that former life.

I thought back to the dream about the little dried out princess from 3000 years ago who the scientists and occultists together managed to resuscitate, and who had been killed by the lid of the jar I was trying to put her in to keep her safe. I now thought of another explanation for that dream. I was being harassed to write the book and to write it in a particular way. Friends (particularly T — though there were others too) were crowding me, unbalancing the delicate and fragile relationship I had with that ancient 'memory' and threatening its destruction. Trance mediumship is a great mystery and by no means as straightforward as most people believe. Who knows what part the vehicle plays and what part the disembodied spirit. If, indeed, there are such things as disembodied spirits! I have always been, and will always be, most cautious about taking messages through mediums — fascinated as I am by the possibilities of the phenomenon.

T now told me that she had known all along I was not a reincarnation of Akhenaten, but had told me that in order to make me write the book. A clear case of manipulation if ever I saw one! Luckily I had not believed her. However, I may not have been Akhenaten himself, but I did seem to have some connection with his life and times, and some energy from this connection seemed to be motivating me in the writing of the book and turning my present life around.

Over the next few years I tried to find a publisher for *The Son of the Sun*. My English agent seemed to be doing nothing for me. Neither did my agent in America. I was in despair and T suggested she should be my agent 'as a friend'. I felt uneasy about this, but, as always, I found it difficult to say 'no' to T.

On 15 November 1983 my English agent had lunch with an editor at Arrow. He was looking for a good fantasy writer. My agent suggested me and told him she would send him my "Tall Stones" trilogy. The very next day, 16 November 1983, T had lunch with the same editor because he was publishing a book about astrology written by her. She told him about my Egyptian book. The coincidence of hearing about me from two people in one week roused his interest.

Then followed a very awkward time for me. Both my English agent and T claimed to have found a publisher for me.

At one point the tug between the two of them to represent me became very stressful. I decided against T when she began to hint that I would never get it published without her and her spirit's help. I began to have sleepless nights, afraid to reject her spirits, having sunk so low in my own estimation of myself at that time that I believed I was entirely dependent on them for my writing ability. My husband pointed out that I had been inspired to write books before I met T, and that "Guardians of the Tall Stones", written long before I met her, was accepted as a major and profound work. (Published first in 1976, it is still in publication in the year 2007.)

Both Oliver and the film star, Diane Baker, who for a few years in the eighties was interested in making a film of my "Tall Stones" and had become a good friend, advised me to stay with the professional agent. T told me to go 'into the silence' and ask my spirits. I returned home by bus, in tears, and heard the phone ringing as I turned my key in the door. It was Dennis Barrett (the psychic healer who had healed me of angina in 1976). He never phoned me. But just this moment he felt the urge to do so. I poured my problem out to him over the phone and he and his spirits said unequivocally I must stay with my professional agent. I knew intuitively this was right.

The editor at Arrow in fact turned down *The Son of the Sun*. He wanted a new fantasy novel for his list, hinting that he might take *The Son of the Sun* if the new one was successful. I discussed an idea I had to write a novel about the dark knight that kept cropping up in the Arthurian stories. But he didn't want that. He wanted a story about a menacing dark tower. I wrote *The Tower and the Emerald* for him.

I had such difficulty in trying to find a publisher for *The Son of the Sun* that I wondered if it had something to do with T who had said I would not get it published without her help.

I consulted my other psychic friend, Meryt, and she suggested we tried a method of disentangling oneself from oppressive influences described in a book by Phyllis Krystal: *Cutting the Ties That Bind*. By coincidence on the way to do this with Meryt, the car I was in stopped in a traffic jam beside a huge sprayed-on graffiti which said "The Eternal Triangle".

The method involves you visualising a triangle of light, the peak of which represents the Higher Consciousness. On the ground you visualise two circles touching each other joined by a flowing line of light that forms a figure eight. You place yourself in one of the circles, and the person you want to cut from in the other.

On Saturday 27 July 1985 we went to a lecture by Phyllis Krystal, and the next day Meryt guided me through the process of cutting the ties from T.

It was an amazing visualisation involving a pure quartz-crystal, brilliant and translucent, focusing the light from the Higher Consciousness down from the Apex of the triangle. T, standing in one circle, was staring at me with those amazing hypnotic eyes of hers. When I put dark glasses on her influence was reduced. I cut the threads that were holding my fingers to hers, indicating that her manipulation of my writing had been cut.

Meryt saw a huge snake wound around her body, and I saw dozens of small snakes wriggling towards me. Meryt advised a ring of fire to intercept them. The snakes were interpreted as T's tempting me to embrace fully the occult life. A few weeks before I had been tormented by obscene phone calls and I was tempted to curse the man on the end of the line. I did not. But the temptation was there. As soon as I recognised the snakes they retreated like a film wound backwards. They dissolved into grey ash and were blown away.

At last in 1986 my book *The Son of the Sun* was published by a small but reputable firm in London, Allison & Busby.

In June 1986, when it was about to be published, another strange incident took place connected with it.

I was travelling up to town on a bus and was carrying a protea from Cape Town. I sat next to a woman who remarked on the flower. We talked about general matters until she was about to get off the bus. Just as she rose to go she asked if I believed in reincarnation. I said I was a writer whose books presupposed the existence in reincarnation. She asked for a name of one of my books and I scribbled the name "Guardians of the Tall Stones" on a piece of paper. We parted.

A few days later I had a letter from her via Arrow, the publisher of my "Tall Stones" series. It turned out she lived quite near to me. She suggested we might meet again. We arranged that she and two friends who were staying with her should come to tea with me. I confess at this stage I was not very keen to take up my time with strangers, but changed my mind when she told me that Winifred Franklin, one of her friends, had said when she was told she was going to visit me: 'I used to speak with the pharaohs you know.' This startled me as up to this time no mention of Egypt had been made between us. They came on Wednesday 11 June 1986. Joyce and her friend Elsie had been nurses during the war, on the front line in Egypt and Italy, like my sister Joan.

As soon as they entered the room I felt our meeting was somehow important. Almost immediately Winifred looked over my shoulder and said that she saw an Egyptian standing behind me with rays of the sun coming down around us. 'You are a daughter of the Sun', she said, 'and he wants you to know you have been chosen to write the true story of his life.'

'Who is he?' I asked, stunned.

I had not mentioned my Egyptian book though it was to be published that week and I had received an advance copy that very day, 'Akhenaten,' she replied.

Winifred was getting as excited as I because she had been told some years ago by 'the pharaohs of Upper Egypt' (she didn't name them and I suspect she didn't know much academically about Egyptian history) that a writer was coming who would speak for them. She'd been looking for this writer for years. She felt she had been led to me to reinforce my confidence and resolve in this important task. She told me Akhenaten was saying that I had two more to write — but whether this meant two more books about him, or two more about ancient Egypt, she wasn't clear. As it happened I did write two more books about ancient Egypt — but I also wrote two more versions of the original *Son of the Sun*.

As she was leaving, Winifred held my hand. I shut my eyes and felt a very strong tingling throughout my body and a very strong feeling of Presence. I felt enclosed in light and love and approval and felt I really could write the books 'they' wanted. As I opened my eyes she spoke a beautiful prayer, thanking God for our meeting. I felt very strongly that she was an honest and genuine medium. I had no after-taste of fear and unease as I had with some others.

In the evening, cooking dinner for my family, I knew I had to write the story of Ankhesenpaaten, Akhenaten's daughter. I felt Akhenaten had regretted something in connection with her and wanted to make it up to her in some way.

The next morning as I woke from a strange dream these words wrote themselves:

I am a survivor. I have survived my father and my mother,
my eldest sister (ah, Merytaten!), three husbands, my
children and two revolutions. I walk now in the blood of the
sunset and wonder if I will ever die.

I knew it was Ankhesenpaaten speaking and I would write her story next. The novel would be called *Daughter of Ra*.

But first I wanted to enjoy the publication of *The Son of the Sun*. With so much encouragement from high places I felt sure the book would be a success.

But it was not to be.

Allison & Busby were in serious financial difficulties before they took me on, and within a very short time the receivers moved in and my book ceased to circulate. I was as bitterly disappointed as any author would be. I had had such bad luck trying to get it published and, having finally done so, I couldn't believe there were perfectly ordinary reasons for its demise. I began to have an uneasy feeling that the powerful dark forces represented by the priests of Amun in my book were trying to block the book.

On 10 August 1986 I asked Meryt to help me cut the ties between the Priests of Amun (if they indeed still existed!) and my book, using the triangle and the two circles as we did with T.

We did the ceremony, setting up the triangle of light leading to the Higher Consciousness and the two circles of light on the ground touching to form a figure eight. In one circle I visualised myself, and in the other, the book.

I visualized Noel Street where the office of my publisher had been.

Meryt suggested I call on the one who was blocking the book to come out of the entrance. This I did.

I watched the narrow dark doorway. Suddenly, startlingly, a black and bristling wild boar came charging out and ran off down the street, snorting.

(At the time I was puzzled about this as I did not associate boars with ancient Egypt. But some months later I read in George Hart's book: *A Dictionary of Egyptian Gods and Goddesses* (pub. RKP 1986. *p.*197):

In the Book Of The Dead the sun god instructs Horus to look at a black boar (i.e. Seth), which causes such a violent sensation in the god that he loses consciousness.

Meryt said at once that I must stop it. I must not let it get away to harm me in the future.

I tried shouting after it as I ran, but I knew it was hopeless.

Suddenly Djehuti (Thoth, the Egyptian god of scribes) appeared at my side. He reached out his right hand and the boar stopped clumsily and it seemed as though it was being dragged back unwillingly towards us by an invisible force coming from Djehuti's hand.

It was brought right back until it was standing in front of me. I now felt there was someone on my left side.

Meryt was telling me to demand that whoever was disguised as a boar should reveal him or herself to me.

I demanded — but nothing happened.

I asked for help.

Simultaneously Djehuti and Menkha, Meryt's spirit guide,

on either side of me, pointed at the boar. Another triangle was thus created — the lines of power from their fingers reaching the beast.

Suddenly the creature disappeared and in its place was a tall and arrogant figure of a man. He had blue-black skin. He wore an Egyptian kilt and headdress. His chest and arms were bare. His clothing was gold, blue and white. (Later I realised these were the colours of my book. The inner cover is black. The dust jacket blue and gold. The paper white.)

The figure, as everything else in this scene, seemed extraordinarily and powerfully real. I believed the source of its energy came from the time of Akhenaten — and probably was a manifestation of the priests of Amun who had opposed and overthrown him. They did not want my book to be read.

Meryt told me to look the sorcerer in the eye and demand that he release the book, or be destroyed.

'Remember,' she said, 'light always wins over darkness.'

'Maybe in eternity,' I thought, but I was doubtful that it did in temporal life.

'He is the shadow side of yourself. You have created him. You must look him in the eye.'

'I can't!' I wailed. 'I need help.'

Suddenly a burning, whirling dynamic sun disk with wings appeared, releasing a 'laser' beam of white light that shot straight down, pierced through the top of my head and shone out with incredible force through my two eyes towards the sorcerer.

As the two beams touched him he melted instantly and all that was left of him was a mess of tarry substance with some molten gold. Djehuti and Menkha held my arms and steadied me.

The book lay open before me — the pages fluttering like white doves. I was conscious of a tremendous relief.

Then I began to realise how extraordinary the whole experience was. I swear it did not feel like imagining or dreaming. It felt actual! I truly believed I was standing in Noel Street — cars passing — a white van — people sitting at the cafe on the corner — and all this was happening — black boars, ancient Egyptian magician priest — laser beams — the lot!

Meryt guided me to a visualisation of the seashore and suggested I plunge in and wash myself thoroughly. I was then to burn my old clothes before I put on new ones. I saw tarry stuff oozing out of the fire.

We thanked the Higher Consciousness, and returned to her living room.

We opened our eyes. For a long time we said nothing but just sat silently, shaken.

And then she asked me for a number. I said 27, without thinking. We opened *The Son of the Sun* to page 27 and read the words:

> '...my mind gradually clearing of Ma-nan's spells... my own mind taking over.'

It was from the scene when Djehuti-kheper-Ra makes the first desperate break with the dark priests — for which they never forgave him.

Then Meryt shuffled her Egyptian divination cards and got number 54.

Number 54 depicted two djed columns — Djehuti and Menkha — our supporters and strengtheners. The djed represents strength and support. Meryt always uses the djed as the symbol for her spirit guide Menkha.

When I returned home I heard from my daughter that Winifred had phoned me. She is the medium who saw Akhenaten in my living room and gave me messages from him... She had never phoned me before. She did not phone me ever again. It seemed significant to me that she should try to contact me at the precise moment I was having this 'experience'.

The following day, 11 August 1986, Meryt phoned to say that after I left she had found, by 'chance', an old paper she had not seen for years, describing an extraordinary incident in Egypt. It seems that in 1909, Arthur Weigall (an archaeologist) and Joseph Lindon Smith (an artist accompanying the archaeologists in Egypt to record their findings) planned to put on a play in the form of an invocation, calling 'Akhenaten from the Land of Silence'. It was to be performed in the magnificent rock amphitheatre of the valley in which the ancient Queens of Egypt were buried. The audience was to consist mostly of archaeologists and their families.

Early in the dress rehearsal a sudden and terrible storm occurred in the valley, sending all, audience and performers alike, scattering for shelter. The play was never performed; the wives of Weigall and Lindon Smith who were to play the lead roles both became seriously ill.

'These forces are very real and very dangerous,' Meryt said. 'We must be very careful.'

Several years passed before I could get the book back into print, but strange 'coincidences' and events continued to happen in connection with it. Many of them occurred when I was with my friend Meryt. We had found that we could more easily encounter other realities when we were together — when we joined forces as it were — than when we tried to do so alone. Often, when we were chatting about ordinary day to day matters we would suddenly both feel simultaneously that everything in the room around us was getting further and further away. At such times we felt as though we were contained in a silent bubble, isolated from our everyday world. In this state special thoughts and visions came to us. I called it 'going into the Silence'.

I asked Menkha if I could be given the name of my Spirit guide. He said it was Djehuti (Thoth) the ancient Egyptian god of scribes, the watcher, the recorder. He is symbolised in ancient Egyptian iconography by the sacred ibis bird and the baboon — both natural forms of which had featured in my childhood growing up in South Africa. I had puzzled about why the baboon was considered sacred, but was told the Egyptians had watched troops of baboon gathered to watch the rising of the sun and, at its rising, leaping up and down with apparent excitement.

Strangely it was a baboon that had saved the lives of my husband and myself during a visit to South Africa in 1983. We were on Chapman's Peak route in the Cape, which is built close against a mountain with a tremendous drop into the sea below on the other side. We paused to take a photograph of a baboon sitting on a ledge and, by doing so, escaped a murderous rock fall. I remember laughing at the time and saying that the baboon must have been my guardian angel in disguise.

On 9 September 1986 I again went 'into the Silence' with Meryt. I seemed to be walking through an incredibly fine, light, golden mist.

When I emerged from it I was in Akhetaten (Akhenaten's city) moving down the main street to the Temple. Pylons. Fluttering penants. I went in. I saw a tall, thin, bald priest kneeling before a sun altar in a huge otherwise empty courtyard, his arms raised touching the two nearest corners of the altar. I seemed to hear his thoughts. There was a feeling of everything ending, too soon and too precipitously. There was the agony of frustration because he had tried to achieve something and he was not being allowed to finish what he had started. He was determined to come back to earth to try again. What was it? I had the impression that the religion of which he was priest was good, but not good enough. Something was missing and he, on the verge of finding it, was being snatched away.

An angry mob entered the courtyard at this point, killed the man, and then set about destroying the important parts of the temple.

I found myself back in the golden mist.

This time I emerged in Hatshepsut's temple at Deir el Bahri. There was a priest-scribe seated cross-legged in a small dark room deep in the temple writing frantically by the flickering light of two small terracotta oil lamps. He seemed to be trying to record something before he was prevented.

His name was called. He went out, writing brush still in hand, blinking in the blazing sunlight after the dim room. A group of angry people attacked him, beating him to death. As he lay dying I was aware of his thoughts, his anxiety that 'they' would find what he had been writing and destroy it.

The next time I emerged from the golden mist I saw a nineteenth century gentleman-archaeologist frantically searching through the ruins of Hatshepsut's temple as though he knew that there were some important records there. He was secretive as though he knew something the other archaeologists didn't know.

Meryt asked me to ask the Higher Consciousness, as represented by her spirit guide and mine, to tell us what it was that he was seeking, that the others were trying to find and record.

I was told: 'You cannot be given it. It has to come to you during the effort of seeking.' And then: 'Through your books you are being given another chance to find it. Do not shrink from it. Remember how unexpectedly life can end. Don't waste a day.'

When the Silence ended Meryt and I opened a book at random. This time it happened to be page 107 of *Her-Bak: Egyptian Initiate* by Isha Schwaller de Lubicz (pub. Inner Traditions, 1978).

'It is for you to speak,' said the master, 'Say what is in your heart. Let us hear what thoughts have come to you.'
'Every insight worth having has to be individually won.'
'There is much that is lost and hidden — but finding it is not enough — it has to be given a new and vibrant form through your own understanding that it may illuminate a new age.'

On 12 September 1986 my editor at Arrow said at last he would consider publishing *The Son of the Sun*.

I wondered if my luck had turned after cutting the ties from T and the Priests of Amun.

But he did not want it as it was. He wanted an ancient Egyptian trilogy with *The Son of the Sun* as one of the three. I suggested documenting the rise and fall and rise again of the power of the Priests of Amun through the three stories.

The narrator in the original Allison & Busby edition of *The Son of the Sun* spoke with the voice of Smenkhkare who, at that time, I believed to be the half-brother of Akhenaten and the mysterious unidentified body in tomb 55. But in the interval between the first and second publication I had been doing a great deal more research into the Eighteenth Dynasty and began to be unsettled in my conviction that my protagonist was who I originally thought he was. Several Egyptologists, namely J.R. Harris and Julia Samson, had made a convincing case for his not existing as a separate person, but the name 'Smenkhkare' being the name taken by Nefertiti when she came to the throne briefly after Akhenaten's death.

At first I resisted the idea, not wanting to change my book.

One winter evening, just before closing time at the British Museum, I was walking through the Egyptian gallery pondering this problem. I asked for guidance. When I got home I found a letter from Arrow saying that they would only publish if I worked on it again, making it longer. I took this as a sign. If I had to work on it again I would perhaps receive guidance as to whether to go with the new theory or not. As it happened I remembered that the story of the nameless oracle had come to me without the name Smenkhkare attached, and that nothing of importance in the deeper meaning of the book would be lost if he now had a different name. The name Djehuti-Kheper-Ra that came to me was more than satisfying symbolically. Djehuti — the watcher, the recorder. Kheper, transformation. Ra, the Sun.

I did not, after all, set out to solve the mystery of Akhenaten, but to show how his story is still very much active in the world, and the inspiration of his life will always be paramount when a religion becomes stale and corrupt and needs a new and vigorous approach.

On 16 October 1986 I had another crisis of doubt about my books. Meryt opened books 'at random' to get messages.

The Mythic Tarot, p.55:

Behind the wheel stand the Moirai, and there is an intelligent and orderly plan behind the apparently random changes in life.

I was named for the Moirai, the ancient Greek Fates, and Meryt felt this was a propitious sign.

Sphinx by Robin Cook, *p.17* (the passage describes entering Tutankhamun's tomb for the first time):

…trying to see what was there without disturbing the dust. Dust already having been disturbed somewhat by their entering the tomb and flying around in the air…

This seemed appropriate. I was trying to see what was there without disturbing the dust. I remembered that when the first person touched the apparently perfectly preserved body of the mysterious figure in tomb 55 it disintegrated into dust. I did not want to do this with my writing.

Her-Bak, Vol.1, *p.344*:

This passage spoke about the dismantled blocks from Akhenaten's temple at Karnak being used for another temple at another time.

Later, in the book *Tombs, Temples and Ancient Art* by Joseph Linden-Smith, we again opened to a page where he was speaking about dismantled blocks from one temple being re-assembled and re-used for another temple.

I interpreted the message from these passages thus:

In my writing I was using the genuine original blocks, but reassembling them with my twentieth century insights for twentieth century readers. This is acceptable — the symbols carved on the blocks are universal and eternal, appropriate for any time and place.

On 21 November 1986, Meryt saw 'in the Silence' a huge figure beside me putting an Egyptian writing palette and reed down on the table in front of me. And then from another group of figures who were surrounding us one slammed down a huge golden ankh. We both felt incredible power emanating from the ankh, and were told that the Copts in Egypt had identified it with the Christian cross and this was acceptable as it was the symbol for eternal life and not limited to any one dogma.

The book we opened 'at random' this time gave us:

The priest (holding out an ankh) now stands aside and indicates that you should proceed within. You find that your earlier fears have left you with the touch of the ankh and that you are eager to discover what lies within. You enter through a narrow stone door... with the symbol of life in your hand you go forward unafraid... Time, also, seems without meaning here...

In early June 1987 I met a stranger in Glastonbury who told me how he and a friend had been alone in the King's chamber of the Great Pyramid when they were young, fooling about, without reverence. His friend climbed into the sarcophagus and he positioned himself to take a photo. Suddenly he was hit by what felt like an electric shock. On leaving the pyramid he found himself so tired he could barely walk. Once in bed he slept for days and during that time had a vivid and detailed dream of initiation. Later he realised he had been standing at dead centre of the pyramid at noon on the 21 June.

On 24 April 1988 I was in Paris, visiting the Egyptian galleries at the Louvre. I found an ancient Egyptian mirror in the shape of Hathor's head. I found myself staring at my reflection. Behind me I was startled to see the figure of Hathor, the goddess of birth and life, also reflected. She seemed to be compelling me to look at myself although I wanted to turn away. Behind me I saw other faces stretching back and back as though to infinity. 'This is one who has great potential,' Hathor said, 'who has the weight of many lives behind her, who is favoured by the gods... yet this is one who procrastinates, who finds excuses not to fulfil her destiny, who seeks the comfortable way...'

My eyes filled with tears of shame and I could no longer see the images in the mirror. When I had blinked them away, the mirror was blank, except for my own face. (This incident I used in chapter 7 of *The Son of the Sun*.)

On 7 May 1986 I was trying to write the additions to *The Son of the Sun* to meet the new publisher's deadline, and finding it very hard to do.

At 3 a.m. I woke and knew I should get up and write — but did not want to. I went back to sleep. After I had been woken three times I said petulantly, 'If you want the book written — you write it!'

Immediately I sat bolt upright, wide awake, and words were clamouring in my head to be written. I could scarcely get them down fast enough. This is what was written (later, most of this was included in Chapter 5 of *The Son of the Sun*):

> Ah, gentle faced Son of the Sun, pacing the flowery halls and passageways of your palace, sleepless in the night, heart bursting with all the great dreams for your people. You see them as purged and purified of all false expectations, freed from superstition and fear, released from heavy obligations to greedy and corrupt priests. You see all the people of the world, from boy working the water-bucket at the irrigation canal to the noble sculptor modelling the divine features in plaster and chiselling them in stone, united in joy and love, the one light shining into their hearts, the one light making them see. From the first cry of the child at birth to the last sigh of the dying man you hear only one theme — praise of the great force that drives them all to fulfil one mighty and magnificent purpose.
>
> Akhenaten believes the world is a perfect place, made imperfect by the separation between people, the divisions and rivalries, the struggle to assert the part against the whole, the petty and temporary self against the great and eternal self. He wants to draw all living beings together into his own body as it were, and with that body, now transformed into a pure and holy channel, mediate the Light of the First and Last, the one and the only, so that all may be nourished by it, all sustained and ennobled and transformed by it.
>
> As he stands in the great Temple, open to the sky, and lifts his arms to the Aten, he is lifting the arms of all mankind, he is lifting every heart, every dream, every aspiration. With

such a common and overwhelming purpose how can brother steal from brother, brother envy brother, brother murder brother?

The palace is built for light. There are more window spaces along the upper walls than there ever have been in any building before. Light pours down and illuminates with dazzling brilliance the painted scenes of fish swimming among water lilies, birds among trees, gazelle peacefully cropping. There are more garden courtyards, stair-wells open to the sky, and chambers open to the flow of people to and from than in any other palace.

For Akhenaten the Aten has no shadowy secrets, no dark side, no hidden and dangerous elements. 'Love the Aten through me' he says, 'and all that will follow will be pure and beautiful as it was meant to be at the Beginning.'

He sleeps little, his thoughts crowding and teeming with all his plans to change the human race. Many a night he bursts into my sleep-chamber and, talking volubly, his face alight with his vision, he pours out his ideas, pacing back and forth, back and forth, hardly aware of me wearily propped up on an elbow watching him, longing for him to go so that I can go back to sleep. Often I am ashamed of my impatience, of my unworthy doubts, of my lack of faith that the human race can and will change.

'Don't you see,' he ways, ' it is because we have had so many different gods, each with its rival demands that we are always in conflict with one another. When we have one overwhelming and overriding belief and are all working with one aim in mind, conflict with cease.'

'Ay,' I think. 'It is a fine dream, but how long will it be before the conflict starts again between those who think the Aten should be worshipped in this way, and those who think it should be worshipped in that? How long before one thinks he is nearer to the Aten and another that he is?' Sometimes I think it is in the rich variety of life and the flight of the soul through the forest of experience that most surely leads us to a sense of the numinous and a belief in a beautiful and cosmic purpose.

On 17 January 1988 I spent the day (after many such days) struggling to write the extra hundred pages I had to add to *The*

Son of the Sun for it to be accepted for the Amun trilogy by Arrow. I was finding it difficult. Indeed I was totally blocked. After a wasted day (and I *hate* wasting days) at four o'clock I was lying on my bed almost in tears — totally depressed about my writing ability. The phone rang. It was Meryt, my very great friend. She said, 'I've just received an SOS call to phone you.' This call was from the spirit world! It was extraordinary. I poured out all my problems. Just the fact of doing so made me feel better and ready to tackle the book again. Also the confirmation that all those strange levels of being really do exist was timely.

In 1990 *The Son of the Sun* was published by Arrow UK as the middle volume of an ancient Egyptian trilogy.

It almost immediately sold out as soon as it was published. The publishers did not choose to reprint. The publishing firm was in the process of change, being absorbed into a larger body. So once again the book I'd been told to write, and that had come to me so strangely and powerfully, was out of print.

Throughout the years all this was happening I had been writing other books, many of them with strange events of their own to accompany the writing. Disappointed in what had happened to *The Son of the Sun* I gave up thinking about Akhenaten and concentrated on my other writing.

But more was to come.

In 1994 I received a letter from a man who said he had found a copy of my book *The Son of the Sun* in a second hand bookshop in Ireland. It had, he claimed, 'blown his mind' and he wanted to meet me.

Egyptologists do not know what happened in the end to Akhenaten. He disappeared, his body has never been found, and his successors did everything in their power to eliminate all record of him from history. In my book I suggested that he had been assassinated by the Priests of Amun whose power he had attempted to break. In my book he was thrown into the desert, spells being said over his body to prevent him being reborn or taking his rightful place in the great solar barque among the stars. The man who wrote to me (whom I will call D.K.) said that he had met a Bedouin in Egypt who had met the ghost of Akhenaten wandering in the desert and claiming that the Priests of Amun had murdered him and cast a holding spell upon his soul so that he was doomed forever to walk the earth and progress no further.

I was invited to meet D.K. and, intrigued, accepted.

There followed an extraordinary afternoon. I sat almost mesmerized as D.K. poured out fascinating and bizarre theories one after the other, about most of which he swore me to secrecy. The one that affected me was that he believed utterly that Akhenaten was in fact trapped as a ghost in the desert, and that it was our duty, our destiny, to travel to Egypt, do battle with the Priests of Amun who had imprisoned him, reverse the spell and release him. As he talked my eyes must have shone with excitement. Yes! That is what I must do!

I returned home, determined to do this, and told my family about it.

It was my son Julian who made me think again. He spoke quite sharply to me, like a parent to a child.

'Mother, when are you going to get off the fence? Either what you believe is true — in which case what you propose to do is extremely dangerous. Or it is not — in which case it is pointless. If it is true — what makes you think you would be able to defeat Beings so powerful that they have held a mighty pharaoh in thrall for three millennia?'

I bit my lip and was silent. He was right.

On 21 April 2001, coincidentally, the post that brought me this piece about going to Egypt with D.K. to lift the curse on Akhenaten to correct from Serena, who is typing it for me, also brought me a book by Dominic Montserrat: *Akhenaten: History, Fantasy and Ancient Egypt* (Routledge, 2000). His book sets out to document the amazing interest in Akhenaten over the past century. His bibliography stretches to thirteen closely packed pages, and his list of literary treatments of Akhenaten to three and a half. He lists *The Son of the Sun* in the section about Akhenaten as a representative of an alternative religion, and quotes only from the blurb: "Moyra Caldecott had her interest in the paranormal confirmed in recent years by her own strange experiences under hypnosis, as a result of which Son of the Sun was conceived." It made me wish I had not revealed anything about the writing of it to the public. If I had not, he might have included my book among the "Literary Akhenatens" instead of among "the nutty fringe" writers.

Reading his book made me think again about writing this autobiography. Should not the stories I have written be left to stand on their own? Is it not detracting from the stories to show the cogs and wheels and pieces of string that make them work and hold them together?

Montserrat states the premise of his book on the first page:

> Akhenaten-themed theologies, paintings, novels, operas, poems, films, advertisements, fashion accessories and pieces of domestic kitsch have all been created. This book is the first attempt to look at them and try to understand why their makers chose Akhenaten. I want to know what interests are served, at particular historical moments, by summoning up the ghost of a dead Egyptian King.

(In a sense I had the same question in mind when I chose to write my latest novel *The Ghost of Akhenaten*, but I was sidetracked by the adventure story and never really answered the question.)

Montserrat suggests, and I agree with him, that every book written is written from the point of view of the writer no matter how objective he or she tries to be. I believe that that point of view of the writer is an integral part of the power of the story. In this autobiography it will become clear that my interest is in much more than "the ghost of a dead Egyptian king".

II: *Hatshepsut: The Daughter Of Amun*

The story of Hatshepsut, the daughter of Pharaoh Thutmosis I, widow of the Pharaoh Thutmosis II, and step-mother/aunt of Pharaoh Thutmosis III. Not content to be regent for her young stepson/nephew on her husband's death — she took the double crown of Egypt and ruled as pharaoh herself, wearing the costume and false beard of a male king on state occasions. During her reign the priests of the god Amun were promoted to positions of considerable power and the temple that still today brings gasps of admiration from tourists was built against the mountain cliffs of Deir el Bahri. No one knows how she met her end — but when she disappeared from history her name was cut out of her buildings, her statues were smashed and the royal lists of Egypt made no mention of her.

I had always been fascinated by ancient Egypt, but it wasn't until the early 1970s that I became interested in Hatshepsut, the female pharaoh who usurped the throne from the legitimate heir and ruled Egypt as forcefully as any man for many years.

I had set *The Tall Stones* stories and *The Lily and the Bull* in the Bronze Age, round about 1500-1450 BC. Hatshepsut reigned c.1473-1458 BC. It seemed to me as I spun the ancient British stories that Hatshepsut was always in the background. In chapter 11 of *Lily and the Bull* I mentioned her haunting a sacred grove in Crete. I read somewhere that some scholars believed Hatshepsut's mother was from Minoan Crete, and married to Thutmose I. It was common for Egyptian pharaohs to marry foreign princesses, so I believed it.

Although the four novels of the "Guardians of the Tall Stones" series are set in ancient Britain, there is much talk of Egypt (or Gypta as I call it in the books). Several of the characters have past lives connecting them with Egypt, and Khu-ren, Kyra's husband, actually came from there in his present life. When Deva comes under the influence of the powerful practitioners of black magic, brings about her mother's death and almost destroys the Temple of the Sun, the ex-High Priest Guiron was called upon to help erase their dark teaching from the girl's mind. In 1982 I had stood on the cliff edge above Hatshepsut's temple at Deir el Bahri and had gazed across the river towards Karnak. I imagined I caught a glimpse of flashes of light from the gold tips of the obelisks in the Temple of Amun there, though I knew they had long since disappeared.

From *The Silver Vortex* (chapter 22):

Guiron stood at the edge of the cliff overlooking Hatshepsut's temple. He could see the flat flood plain, greening towards the sinuous muscular thread of the Nile and fading back to the ochre colour of the desert before it reached the faint pink smudge of the distant eastern mountains. Exhaustion and hunger had gone beyond agony and he seemed to be poised above the landscape, contained in a kind of timeless fiery ball of heat.

The huge orb of the sun was sinking behind the mountains of the west, but before it went, its long rays touched the golden tips of the obelisks and rods of blinding light sprang out from them.

Through the power of Guiron's mind these beams shot out across the world, swifter than thought itself, to where Deva stood.

She had asked for help to forget Urak's teaching, and this was the only way. It was being burned out of her memory once and for all. After this there would be no lingering seed to grow again another time. The knowledge would be lost to her for ever.

Deva rejects her evil mentors after this and asks her father if she may return to Egypt to work out her penance. She appears under the name she had used in a former Egyptian life, Anhai. She is a fictional character studying to be a healer in the historical novel I wrote about Hatshepsut.

It was as far back as June 1977 that I was seriously contemplating writing a novel about Hatshepsut herself.

On 17 August I awoke determined to write a novel about Hatshepsut, and told my husband about it excitedly at breakfast. At noon Oliver phoned me from the office to say he had just received an advance promotional leaflet for a novel about Hatshepsut written by Pauline Gedge, *The Child of the Morning*. I gave up in despair. I was too late. She was a much better known author. My book didn't stand a chance.

After Arrow had published my "Guardians of the Tall Stones", *Silver Vortex* and *The Tower and the Emerald*, they finally agreed to publish my Egyptian novel, *The Son of the Sun*, but only if I made it longer and wrote two other novels to make it part of a trilogy.

Oliver persuaded me that anything I wrote would be very different from anything Pauline Gedge wrote. Every incident in the lives we are currently living is so complex it can be described and interpreted in many different ways. How much more so a life from 3000 years ago about which we know only fragments!

I decided I would write about Hatshepsut after all.

I described to the editor at Arrow how I should write this novel:

1. Because Arrow are promoting me as a Fantasy writer and not as a writer of historical fiction, I could write it to match my other rather mystical/magical novels. It would however have an historical framework. Egypt has been called 'the home of magic' and I have already made quite a study of the esoteric meaning of their myths and their religion. Hatshepsut herself was a strange mixture of the 'psychic' and the 'practical'. She was ambitious, ruthless, worldly — but also a High Priestess of the Mysteries — and her temple at Deir el Bahri is constructed and decorated in such a way as to portray the deepest teachings of her religion.

2. I could write the Hatshepsut novel as another in the "Guardians of the Tall Stones" series. I would follow Deva's adventures after the end of *The Silver Vortex* when she goes to Egypt to train as a priest. The story of Hatshepsut would then be seen through the eyes of a foreigner from Britain, training at Hatshepsut's temple at Deir el Bahri.

3. I had already written about the pharaoh Akhenaten in *The*

Son of the Sun and could therefore write the new novel about Hatshepsut as part of an Egyptian trilogy. I would have the thread of religion running through.

i) *Daughter Of Amun* (about Hatshepsut and the rise of the priests of Amun.)

ii) *Son of the Sun* (about Akhenaten and the fall of the priests of Amun)

iii) *Daughter of the Sun* (about Akhenaten's daughter who was married to Tutankhamun during the time of the restoration of the power of the priests of Amun.)

What I would be describing would be the continual process of our reaching after a satisfactory understanding of the one big and unanswerable question. Someone arises who is inspired to give us a dynamic and fresh approach to the age-old question. After the initial wonderful and exciting impetus, it becomes embodied in a system. It becomes rigid. It becomes corrupted and misused. A whole hierarchy of people develop a vested interest in keeping it going, even if it has become as useless as the system it supplanted.

And then it is swept away — and a new effort is made to get back to the meaningful roots of true religious experience.

So there is a continual rise and fall, ebb and flow. This applies to politics as well as to religion. As soon as a religion becomes a 'system' and not an inspiration — as soon as religion becomes a struggle for control and power and privilege it loses its mystical quality. It loses its true life-enhancing property and becomes dangerous and death dealing. I decided this would be one of the important messages in my three Egyptian novels — and one that is of great relevance even today.

In June 1986, when I had started writing *Daughter Of Amun*, my daughter-in-law, Serena, invited an Australian friend of hers, Jenni Bolton, to lunch at our house. I talked about Hatshepsut and my latest book. Jenni was personal assistant to the rock star Tina Turner. Tina Turner had been fascinated by ancient Egypt for a long time and a Californian psychic had told her that she was a reincarnation of Hatshepsut. (See *pp.*191-192 of *I, Tina. My Life Story* by Tina Turner with Kurt Loder, pub. William Morrow & Co. N.Y., 1986). Jenni told me that Tina would be interested to meet me.

On 29 June 1986 she sent a limousine to fetch me and Rachel, and we visited her at the house she was renting at that time in Holland Park Road, next door to Lord Leighton's house and museum. We got on well, talking mostly about Egypt.

We began a strange friendship that was almost entirely based on our mutual interest in ancient Egypt, and Hatshepsut in particular. That we had met just at the time I was starting to write about Hatshepsut seemed very significant to both of us.

She told me that since Carol, her psychic in the US, had told her she was Hatshepsut, she had been greatly comforted because suddenly the torments of her life made sense. Ike, whom she equated with Thutmose III, was paying her back by abusing her in this life, for taking the throne, in her earlier life.

After I met Tina I wrote this poem and sent it to her:

HATSHEPSUT — 8 July 1986

From the stone
she gazes.
Neither Time nor sand
has dimmed her vision.
She sees
but cannot speak
The chisel broke her lips...
her nose...
Spite and rage toppled her slender form.
As generations live and die...
she waits... she waits... she waits...
When will it be over
the pain
of seeing
without speech?

Diary entry, 9 July 1986:

6 p.m. Phone call from Tina. She's started reading "Guardians of the Tall Stones" and finds a lot for her in it. I'm so pleased because she doesn't often read. I get the feeling she is very excited about our project and the little pieces of writing I am sending her. In fact she said so. The piece about the statue needed some explanation. I told her how the Egyptians 'opened the mouth' of statues so that they could communicate with the world, and

how Thutmose III had broken the noses and mouths of Hatshepsut's statues in order to take the power of communication from her. Tina at once remarked on how Ike used to hit her on the mouth and nose all the time.

On 14 July we visited the British Museum together. She was stared at and followed, but it was not too bad. I took her to the beautiful head of Hatshepsut in the side gallery downstairs, the one I had once seen with a single red rose placed beside it. She stayed with it a long time, and then we went upstairs. There she was most interested in the wigs. One amusing incident occurred. A boy of about twelve was taking a photograph of a mummy in a glass case and Tina walked in front of it. He shooed her away at once. I smiled to think he was probably the only one in the museum who did not recognise her and how he would have scored with his friends later if only he had taken the photograph.

British Museum with Tina Turner, 14 July 1986

'Hey lady
are you that singer?
Are you Tina Turner?'
No.
No. Not today.
Today you cannot see me.
I walk among the ruins of Egypt.
See that mirror there?
It once held my reflection...
perhaps still does.
That stone jar
held kohl for my eyes...
ground malachite
and lapis lazuli...
This is the wig I wore.
How heavy it was.
Even now I dread the weight.
'But are you a singer?'
Yes. Yes. I am a singer.
But I sing songs
you cannot hear.
I sing songs

for these people
waiting
in the painted coffins.
I sing songs for the lost gods...
for the sand blown palaces...
for the shrivelled lotus
that grows again from seed...
'Sing for us Tina.
Sing for us!
Here among the glass cases
at closing time.
Make this dead place
ring with ancient chants
and hymns.
We are living...
who knows who we once were...
who knows who we will be.'

At five o'clock the gallery warders started herding us all out. This struck me as amusing: the great pharaoh Hatshepsut (let alone the celebrity Tina Turner) being herded out of a gallery of broken shards and pieces of her former glory.

I had that feeling of slipping between realities and times very strongly.

Did I believe Tina was Hatshepsut? At that time I think I did. If there is such a thing as reincarnation, Tina, with her powerful personality and charisma, is a good candidate. I felt I might have been a scribe at the time, contacted now as a familiar employee to write her story.

But another famous star also believes she was Hatshepsut. In chapter II of the biography of the dancer and film star Ann Miller, *Tapping Into The Force* by Maxine Asher, she is told by four mediums that she is a reincarnation of Hatshepsut.

But whatever the explanation of the experience of 'far memory' might be, I for one believe that the life we are living here and now is only a very small part of our whole life... only the tip of the iceberg as it were.

Basically we are a continuum. Each one of us extends well beyond this life, before and after... and each act we do has extension. There are no isolated acts. No acts without cause and effect long beyond the life span that we usually consider to be our lot.

Because we are a continuum — because we continue into the *invisible* — we are in touch with things not always easy to explain. "A wonder is not contrary to nature, but contrary to what we *know* of nature." (John Carey in *A Single Ray of the Sun*).

When people find out that I believe in reincarnation, they ask me: 'What is the point of it if we can't remember our past lives?'

I believe we do remember. Deeply in our subconscious, memories of our past lives are influencing everything we do, and what we do now is influencing everything we will be in the future.

That is one kind of memory. Unconscious memory. Subliminal memory.

But sometimes the memories well up from the unconscious and become conscious.

Diary entry, 21 July 1986:

Jenni brought Tina to my house this afternoon. We sat in my study and talked for a long while. I showed her the pictures I had of Hatshepsut's time. We talked about the format of the book I am writing. Tina is very excited about it as a form of exploration, but says I shouldn't speak to publishers about it yet because they'll try to pin us down and exploit her name. I would be happier anyway to get most of it done before we involve a publisher — so that they won't interfere in the way I want to do it. I told Tina I was still unsure of the format. Either I could write the novel about Hatshepsut "straight" as I intended to do before I met her, or I could write it as a diary documenting what we were discovering about Hatshepsut through our interaction and research.

Tina likes this second idea best. So perhaps that is what we'll do.

As it turned out, I wrote *Daughter of Amun* 'straight', as had been my original intention. But now, years later, in this autobiographical piece, I am documenting the progress of our interaction in the Hatshepsut project.

Diary entry, 21 July 1986:

Early this morning, in the small hours, I woke (as usual) and knew I ought to write something about Hatshepsut. Because I'd had too much wine the previous night and was very tired I turned over to go to sleep again. I dozed off and then jerked awake sure I heard footsteps in the house. I searched, but there was no one there. I wondered if it was a trick on the part of those who are trying to make me write this book. I told Tina — though I hadn't intended to — and she said she also felt there was someone coming up her stairs at about that time and knew there was no one there. She had clutched her amethyst crystal for protection and gone back to sleep.

Diary entry, 24 July 1986:

Visited my friend Meryt.
I told her about Tina Turner and the Hatshepsut connection.
Suddenly we both simultaneously began to get that strange feeling we get when Menkha is near. It's as though an otherworld silence has fallen and our bodies feel insubstantial. Can't describe it properly, but we both know the feeling and it is very strong. We stopped talking and shut our eyes.
As we could 'feel' Menkha was with us ready to communicate, I asked the question that was uppermost in my mind: 'Is Tina Turner Hatshepsut?'
Meryt spoke as though someone was speaking through her. I tried to jot it down but only managed to get some of it.
"Don't ask such a specific question. You cannot, must not translate the physical forms of Tina, Moyra, Meryt into the physical forms of the past — the truth is greater than this. The greater issue is understanding the greater truth — not the lesser. Once it is brought into the personal it's immediately brought into conflict."

Diary entry, 26 August 1986:

These words came to me after one of those strange eerie silences. I'd been reading Hatshepsut's inscriptions about the Punt expedition and on the obelisks at Karnak (in Vol. II. Breasted: *Ancient*

Records of Egypt, pub. Russell & Russell, New York 1906) and I was wondering if she ever felt overburdened by the demands for her obedience from the other-world.

> 'Why should I? Why should I: TRUTH is nothing to me. Maat…the living Horus… my father of the Two Lands and my father of the Sun… all demand of me. I am confined. I am led like a leopard on a golden chain. I cannot step where I want to step, or sleep where I want to sleep. Nor can I make love with whom I want to make love…
>
> 'Is there no burden too big to lay upon my shoulders. You have called me. I have not asked for this.'
>
> 'Ah, daughter — have you not? Have you not pleaded. Have you not walked the night, paced the colonnades of the day…your shadow at your feet…your shadow at your back…your shadow going before? I have heard your cry. I have listened and I have said, my daughter — if it is thy wish to play the leopard, then here is my golden chain that you do not destroy my flock. You bowed your head. You took my chain around your neck.
>
> 'Have I not done. all that you asked? Can I — not now be free?'
>
> 'There is no slavery like the slavery of power. You asked for power. You have power. You cannot have freedom too.'
>
> 'I will break the chain around my neck. I will give up the power. I will leave the golden throne and give the double crown to the boy who slavers for it, to the woman who stands at his side and is sick for want of it. I will walk in the shade and call my love to my side.'
>
> 'And will he come when you are not the king? He is ambitious.'
>
> 'He loves me — not the crown?'
>
> 'And do you love you — and not the crown?'
>
> 'What have I become? A walking crown? Have I no legs, no arms, no breast, no thighs?'
>
> 'Give it up then my daughter. Become no more my chosen one. Be as you wish. Be a peasant who tills the field: a woman who cries in the night because her child has no food.'
>
> 'I will. I will give it up. I have given it up. From this moment on I walk where I will and love who I will.'

(I later worked this in to chapter 11 of *Hatshepsut: Daughter of Amun*.)

As an example of the sort of 'coincidence' that triggers scenes in my novels I will relate the following:

25 September 1986. I took a book out of the Egypt Exploration Society Library by Cyril Aldred called *The Egyptians*. I put it aside to read later.

The last thing I'd written in the Hatshepsut book had been about her visit to an amethyst mine in the desert to find that the miners were rebellious and dissatisfied because of the lack of water at the site.

On 26 September I visited Avebury with Oliver, and Brian Ashley of the Henge Shop, showed us how he dowsed the stones for energy patterns. Oliver bought a pair of copper rods and we tried dowsing ourselves.

For the next two days I was busy with other things but on 29 September I returned to my writing. I was stuck, so I decided not to waste time trying to write when I did not feel like it. I decided to do research instead. I opened the Aldred book for the first time. It fell open to page 158 where I read that pharaohs sometimes functioned as water diviners in the desert when wells had to be dug.

I returned to writing at once. Hatshepsut finds water for the miners by dowsing! (*Daughter Of Amun*, chapter 6).

On 18 October I visited Meryt and we had another one of those sessions when we go into that mysterious silent bubble and ask for an experience or an illumination. I wanted help with my Hatshepsut book.

A very vivid scene unfolded before me. Senmut, the architect of Hatshepsut's great Temple and, I believed, her lover, was carrying an image of an ox on a standard into the inner sanctum of her temple. I felt he was angry with Hatshepsut and her god and was making a deliberate blasphemous gesture. There was an unseemly struggle as the priests with Senmut tried to push forward, and Hatshepsut's priests tried to push them back. I understood his anger had several sources. One was her attitude to his sexuality and this was why he was displaying an ox, which is a neutered bull. He felt she was emasculating him. But he was also unhappy about her obsessive relationship with her god and was trying to make the point that her god was not all that omnipotent if he, Senmut, could storm into the god's sanctuary and go unpunished.

At this point Meryt asked where Hatshepsut was while this was happening. I 'saw' an image of her in bed with another man. She was furious when she heard what Senmut had done and either had him killed or, by removing her favour from him, gave Thutmosis III the opportunity to destroy him. Hatshepsut believed at that point she could do without him — but after his death she was very vulnerable.

I began to feel very uneasy and told Meryt I had had enough. She guided me back to ordinary life in the way Phyllis Krystal suggests — visualizing myself entering water, washing myself thoroughly, and clothing myself in new clothes. I followed her instructions but found myself presented with a long black hooded cloak. Meryt told me to discard it quickly, and to wash myself again. This time I found a light green dress waiting for me.

I wondered about the black cloak and felt that in my whole Egyptian experience I was treading dangerously close to dark forces. I must be *very* careful.

I also wondered about the ox as the symbol chosen to defy Hatshepsut and her god. I looked up various books and read:

Joseph Campbell, *The Mythic Image*, p.32:

The meaning for example of the ass and the ox in the
Nativity scene would in the 4th century AD have been
perfectly obvious to all, since these were the beasts symbolic
in that century of the contending brothers, Seth and Osiris.

Therefore, in the Nativity context, their juxtaposition meant reconciliation.

Note in connection with my image of Senmut and the ox — Osiris was castrated and his phallus was never recovered, after Seth's dismemberment of him.

In J.C. Cooper, *An Illustrated Encyclopaedia of Traditional Symbols*, p.124: 'The ox is dangerous when undisciplined, but powerfully useful when tamed.'

Was Senmut trying to warn Hatshepsut that an undisciplined priesthood with too much power would be dangerous? Or was he just making a personal point about her emasculation of him? Perhaps both these motives were present, plus some others as well. At any rate, I had been given something to think about and a scene for my book. I wrote it into chapter 14.

Other examples of scenes in the book springing from incidents in my own life, are:

My description of the lowering of the incense tree from Punt in the book is based on my watching the replanting of a full grown palm tree in the new Palm House at Kew, London in 1987.

The incident of Hapuseneb walking out of the temple unchallenged with the cosmic egg is based on seeing someone walk out of a College in London where I was studying hieroglyphics, with a box of books. We watched without realising at the time that they were being stolen.

The incident of Hatshepsut putting a hand on a cobra as a child was based on an experience of my own as a child. I was in the Drakensberg in South Africa, and I bent down to pick a flower and felt something move under my hand. It was a deadly poisonous snake.

Several scenes have come to me in those psychically charged sessions with Meryt. I have already mentioned Senmut's sacrilegious procession in Hatshepsut's temple. The scene on Sehel Island with the frangipani flowers is also from one of those sessions, as is the scene when Men-soneb is burned and then confronted with writhing snakes.

On 5 November 1986 in a session with Meryt we saw Hatshepsut as a young girl offering a bracelet of lapis lazuli, turquoise and carnelian on the altar of her god, Amun-Ra. I knew it was a sacrifice for her to give it up as it had been given to her by her father. I saw the shadow of her father watching her. Suddenly a shaft of light accepted the bracelet. She dedicated herself to the service of her god totally. Her father turned and left for the Eternal Realms well satisfied with his daughter.

Suddenly this scene faded and another took its place. This time it was of the Temple as it is now, ruined. I heard mocking laughter from the cliffs. I felt she failed in much that she set out to do in her lifetime and is still struggling to complete her vow.

On 27 August 1987 I had been writing that some of the priests of Ra had supported Thutmosis III, Men-kheper-Ra, in his bid to overthrow Hatshepsut, and today I read in *The Obelisks of Egypt* by Labib Habachi (Dent, 1978) that Thutmosis III erected many obelisks dedicated to Ra, including those at

Heliopolis, the centre of Ra worship, while Hatshepsut dedicated her obelisks to Amun.

Jenni Bolton came to dinner and we discussed the Hatshepsut project. I told her I did not know what kind of book I was supposed to be writing. What kind of role did Tina want to play in it?

Jenni said she thought Tina was serious about her interest in Hatshepsut, but her manager Roger Davies was very against her making too much of it in public. He did not want her being accused of being some kind of nut. Evidently she is very reliant on psychics and he feared I was just another psychic trying to exploit her.

After Jenni left I felt depressed. Arrow were keen for me to involve Tina in the book and for six months I had been working on it believing that she wanted to be part of it.

But this morning I woke with a sense of relief and a sincere hope that she does not want to be part of the book. I would be writing the book just as I would want to, with no one else to consider. I had been worrying how to pitch the book. Her fans would not necessarily like my kind of rather philosophical book, whereas my "readers" might be put off if it was connected with a rock star.

Diary entry, 4 November 1986:

Tina phoned. She wants me to write the Hatshepsut book, but not mention her or involve her. She told me her manager was against her involvement, but any help she could give she would be pleased to give, even to paying my fare to Egypt for research. Then, she said, in 1988 she will be looking for film roles and she would be very interested to play Hatshepsut. She will more than probably buy my book for a film.

Meanwhile I must write it as I see it — no holds barred. I was delighted. This is just what I wanted.

We will meet on Sunday and I will bring the Naville books to show her.

On 16 December she gave me a gold pendant of the god Djehuti — Thoth, the god of scribes. The one Meryt said was my spirit-guide!

Diary entry, 24 December 1986:

Yesterday Oliver was phoned at work by an American author, who said he was writing a book about Hatshepsut helped by Thutmose I, Thutmose II, Thutmose III and Anubis. He asked if Oliver would like to publish it. Oliver told him at once he did not publish fiction, but anyway he could not because his own wife was writing a book about Hatshepsut, helped by Hatshepsut herself. The man sounded quite shocked and said: 'She couldn't have been contacted by Thutmose I, II and III or they would have told me!'

Fascinating. The feud of the Thutmosids continues!

Diary entry, 7 January 1987:

I was phoned by Tina Turner's publicity man, who was preparing the brochure for her "Break Every Rule" world tour and wanted to put two of my books in her list of favourite books. She had suggested *Guardians of the Tall Stones* and *Son of the Sun*.

Diary entry, 16 June 1987:

Tina sent us four tickets to her concert at Wembley, London. Oliver, Rachel, Roger Hammond (in place of Julian who was away) and I went. We had seats very near the front and for several days afterwards I was almost deaf. It was an amazing experience. Tina Turner and I had spent time talking quietly about ancient Egypt, but now she was transformed. We were in a box with lights flashing, music thundering and thousands of people screaming, as well as the woman strutting upon the stage belting out sound that could have stripped paint off a house at 500 metres! Patrick Woodroffe, who was responsible for the lighting, later dined at our house and bought a pastel of Oliver's for his daughter. He played on our emotions with light as savagely as the music did, and 10,000 people were welded into one animal screaming in apparent ecstasy. I believe that if Tina had been within reach she would have been ripped apart, triumphant fans carrying away pieces of her hoping to give their grey little lives some kind of colour and drama. I remembered 'fan' stood for 'fanatic'. The atmosphere was primitive, primal. We were caught in a hurricane of light and sound and movement. We were flung this way and that emotionally. We were played on, assaulted, uplifted, deafened. It was wonderful.

For the rest of 1987 Tina was on world tour and Oliver and I were doing battle with the horrible reality of his cancer. I finished the first draft of both *Daughter Of Amun* and *Women in Celtic Myth* and Oliver told me they were good.

I did not hear from Tina again until 11.30 a.m. on 23 February 1988 when she phoned me from Kuala Lumpur to find out how I was getting on. I told her I had finished the book and she was very excited. She wanted to read it immediately and said she would send a courier for it. She also wanted another copy of *The Son of the Sun*.

On 25 February I was washing dishes in the kitchen when the doorbell rang. I went to the door wiping my hands on my apron. It was a courier from Mick Jagger's office to fetch the manuscript of *Daughter of Amun* for Tina, now in Japan. I sent the following letter.

25 February 1988

Dear Tina,

The book has been written as it came to me. It is not all there is to say about Hatshepsut and there may well be more to come — but I 'felt' it was right to put it down at this point and call it 'complete'.

I had great difficulty at the beginning because I was worried what you would think about it, or what my publisher or the scholarly Egyptologists would think about it — and then I knew I'd never write anything worthwhile if I was looking over my shoulder all the time. So I just plunged in and wrote as it flowed. A lot of the time I held the crystal you gave me and I enclose a photo Oliver took of me holding it.

I apologise for the untidiness of the typescript, but I thought you would rather see it soon than wait weeks for me to retype it. I'm sure it is quite readable as it is.

Diary entry, 3 May 1988:

I had another long call from Tina. She was very enthusiastic about the Hatshepsut book and mentioned going to Egypt with me and Jenni — but when she was rested. She was pretty exhausted after her tour.

On 4 May I delivered a copy of my *Women in Celtic Myth* to Tina at the St. James Club.

In September 1988 Arrow finally accepted the revised and lengthened *The Son of the Sun* and the whole concept of the trilogy involving the book about Hatshepsut.

In early October 1988 I had a phone call from Tina to ask if I would come to Egypt with her and Jenni in a couple of weeks time. I said 'yes' immediately, but stood, stunned, by the phone after I'd put it down. I couldn't believe it would really happen.

But it did.

On 15 October 1988 a huge black limousine came to my front gate to start me on my journey to Egypt with Tina Turner. Family and neighbours gathered to cheer and I felt very unreal as the chauffeur opened the door for me.

With Jenni I waited in the lounge of the St. James Club for Tina to finish her packing. We were served tea in exquisite bone china cups.

I am the sort of person who is always early for an appointment and I grew agitated as I checked my watch and the time for our flight departure grew ever nearer. Jenni was very relaxed, as always, even when I pointed out that there might be traffic hold-ups on the way to the airport.

'Don't fret,' she said. 'They'll hold the plane for Tina.'

In Egypt at Deir el Bahri, Hatshepsut's temple, she was recognised by tourists and was mobbed for her autograph. She would not sign any and we rushed from place to place trying to avoid her persecutors. Later I asked Jenni why she didn't sign a few if only to get rid of them. They were like flies around a jam pot. Jenni said I had no idea how intrusive and aggressive her fans could be. If she gave them an inch they would demand a mile, each believing that she somehow belonged to them. She usually travelled with bodyguards, but with us she had none. She was supposed to be on a private trip, and had dressed down, hoping not to be recognised. I began to lose hope that we would see anything of Egypt at this rate.

But miraculously there was a gap between the departure of one set of coaches and the arrival of another, just as we reached the colonnade where all the most interesting inscriptions about Hatshepsut's conception and birth were depicted on the walls. I had brought translations of all the inscriptions and we sat down on a step and I began to read them to her. I haven't a loud voice, but as I read, it seemed to me I was being taken over by a powerful presence who was intoning the inscriptions through me. Up to this time I think I had believed Tina was indeed Hatshepsut — but suddenly I felt she was not. It seemed to me that Hatshepsut herself was present, speaking through me, trying to get her story told in any way she could — by influencing famous people to believe that they were her, or by influencing writers to write about her… It seemed to me I was her scribe taking dictation from her.

Just as I finished reading the last inscription a new batch of coaches arrived and our peace was destroyed. We fled.

16 October 1988. On the second day Jenni and I went alone to the Temple of Luxor in the morning, but were joined by Tina in the afternoon for a visit to the Temple of Karnak. We dodged fans as best we could and tried to get something of the atmosphere. I showed her where Hatshepsut's image had been scratched out of the reliefs. The Egyptians believed that the image of a person, even a name in inscription, would keep that person's power active in the world. So when she was finally overthrown by Thutmosis III, all her images and names were destroyed. The irony is that those he missed so intrigued the archaeologists millennia later that they sought her out particularly, and she is now more talked about and written about than Thutmosis III himself. I showed Tina Hatshepsut's obelisk, again, ironically, the best preserved in Egypt because Thutmosis had had it bricked up when he was pharaoh. I read her a translation of the inscription.

We returned to the hotel in the late afternoon and I suggested we hire a boat so that we could watch the sunset on the river. Jenni and Tina liked the idea and we retired, arranging to meet again in time for the sunset. Jenni booked a small felucca for three.

Sunset approached. Tina was not ready. I became very agitated and said rather sharply to Jenni that planes might wait for Tina — but the sunset would not. We tired of ringing her room to chivvy her and set off along the corridor to fetch her. She said she was waiting for room service as she had ordered champagne. I insisted we couldn't wait any longer and should go without it.

As we rushed along the corridor towards the lift we met the waiter ambling along holding a silver tray proudly in front of him with champagne, glasses and a crystal vase with a single red rose in it.

We each grabbed something from the tray and left him gasping as we rushed into the lift. Having been so discreet about her presence ever since we arrived, we now went to the opposite extreme and made a huge stir as we rushed through the reception area. I seem to remember being directed through the kitchens as a short cut, then out onto the terrace where the guests were relaxing in deck chairs waiting for the sunset — so spectacular in Egypt.

We hurtled along the path to the river carrying our bottle of champagne and glasses. One of us even had the red rose! The boat Jenni had ordered was too small and Tina insisted that we needed a larger one.

The guests on the terrace watched amused as Tina played the big star. I was embarrassed — but eventually we set sail on the bigger boat and left the hotel behind. The sky was already fire red, but we hadn't missed the best. Jenni poured the champagne and, as I sipped it, I couldn't help thinking how unbelievable it was for me to be drifting down the Nile with a famous rock star sipping champagne!

But then, gradually, I forgot the role I was playing, and Tina forgot the role *she* was playing. Jenni of course, never played a role. She was always herself, a down-to-earth Australian. No sham. No fake. No bullshit.

The incredible beauty of the sky and the water took over. The father and son who crewed the boat were silent and unobtrusive. This was their land and at this moment they were aware of its deep and abiding value.

We began to talk properly to each other for the first time on this trip. Softly, in low and humble voices we discussed what life meant to us, and the possibilities of an after life. The mountains hiding the ancient kings rode beside us. The stars to which they believed they went in death were above us.

When we returned to the hotel landing stage we were very different from the people who had rushed so noisily down the path earlier. We crept onto land in the gathering dark and walked silently to our rooms.

The next day, 18 October, our taxi driver took us to Abydos and Denderah. The Temple at Abydos is still in a remarkable state of preservation, the great hypostile hall still roofed, the only lighting coming in shafts from small windows high against the ceiling. Tina walked in and was caught in one of these shafts as though she were in a spotlight on a stage. But this time she was quiet and subdued and reverent.

The Temple has beautiful wall reliefs of the pharaoh and his gods still bearing the ancient paint, and a king list that omits the names of Hatshepsut and Akhenaten — both regarded as anathema on their deaths and expunged from history. It took more than 3000 years for them to be reinstated by curious and diligent archaeologists.

Denderah is also well preserved and still has the sacred lake, with wind rustling in the palm trees that surround it.

We stood on the roof and looked out over the village on one side and the desert stretching to the far range of mountains on the other. I looked down at the courtyard below us and saw our three shadows imprinted on the dust. The ancient Egyptians believed 'the shadow' was an important one of the nine aspects of the Self. I was musing on this when suddenly a coach load of tourists arrived, and, instantly recognising Tina even from that distance, started to run towards us and scream.

That was the end, yet again, of our peace.

The day we left Luxor we took an early flight so we arrived in Cairo in time to register at the Nile Hilton, while still having time to visit the Museum before lunch. The Museum was supposed to be the jewel in the crown of our visit to Egypt. Tina had been inordinately looking forward to it. But it was a disaster. I remembered our visit to the British Museum in London. We had been watched and followed, but what had seemed oppressive to me there, now seemed the height of good behaviour. Here they shouted at her, and pressed against her, and tried to hold her. She could look at nothing. We moved constantly towards areas that seemed empty, but as soon as we reached them, they were crowded. Faces were pressed close against hers, often with foul smelling breath. And their eyes! What kind of temporary insanity turned people into such hooligans faced with a certain kind of fame?

We fled.

That evening we had one of the better experiences of the journey. We visited the Giza pyramids at night so that Tina could avoid being mobbed by tourists.

There were very few people there and those that were, were locals, mostly young lovers sitting on steps holding hands. No one paid any attention to us. The moon was up, bathing everything in an eerie luminosity. We walked, silently, dwarfed among the gigantic and ancient structures. Somewhere in front of the Sphinx a *son et lumière* programme was running. We benefited by seeing the Sphinx illuminated. Only once the commentary impinged on us and that time it actually enhanced the atmosphere rather than destroyed it. The reverberations of an incantation spoken louder than the rest sounded, mysteriously, to be rumbling from *inside* the king's chamber in the Great Pyramid. I shivered.

III: *Tutankhamun and the Daughter of Ra*

On the disappearance of Smenkhkare (Nefertiti?) and Ay, Akhenaten's young son Tutankhaten was declared pharaoh. To strengthen his position he married his elder half-sister, the daughter of Nefertiti by Akhenaten. This novel is the story of this remarkable young woman. Tutankhamun's fame is assured in the world today because of the riches found in his tomb by Howard Carter and displayed in museum exhibitions throughout the world, but he died at the age of 17 or 18 and it was his wife who had to face the consequences of a dangerous power struggle during which the priests of Amun once again rose to power. Her desperate letters to her country's enemy, the King of the Hittites, still exist, and it is on these that I have based the book of Tutankhamun and the Daughter of Ra.

This is the third in the cycle of novels set in the ancient Egyptian Eighteenth Dynasty.

Akhenaten, the 'heretic' king who tried to revolutionise the Egyptian religious pantheon, and make the Aten, as represented by the disk of the sun, the supreme and only god, has died, probably by assassination. His successors, Smenkhkare and Ay, have also mysteriously disappeared. The young boy, Tutankhaten, his son by a secondary wife, has acceded to the throne, his legitimacy ensured by his marriage to Akhenaten's and Nefertiti's daughter, his half-sister Ankhesenpaaten.

After much political and court intrigue, General Horemheb has gained control over the Two Lands and re-asserted the power of the Priests of Amun. Tutankhaten's name has been changed to Tutankhamun, and his wife's to Ankhesenamun.

The boy king's tomb was discovered in 1922 by the archaeologist Howard Carter and some of the most magnificent artefacts we have from ancient Egypt were found, undisturbed. There cannot be many people alive today who have not heard of Tutankhamun, or seen the objects from his tomb on display in museums or photographed in splendid books. But not so many know the story of his wife, the young Ankhesenamun, facing dangerous and troubled times. Letters from her have been discovered and preserved, telling a story both moving and tragic, but also of daring, intelligence and courage.

This is basically her story — the Daughter of Ra.

At 3 a.m. one morning in June 1986 I half woke and reached for the pen and paper that is always beside my bed. Without being aware of what I wrote I let words flow out of my sleep. When I was fully awake this is what I read:

> I am a survivor. I have survived my father and my mother, my eldest sister, three husbands, my children and two revolutions. I walk now in the blood of the sunset and wonder if I will ever die.

I knew it was Ankhesenamun speaking and I would write her story.

There is some evidence that Ay, Nefertiti's father, succeeded Smenkhkare, and Ankhesenpaaten was married to her grandfather to give his reign legitimacy, and then married to her half-brother Tutankhaten, when Ay died. Her first marriage was to her father, Akhenaten.

By the time I came to write *Daughter of Ra* I was already well steeped in the history of the Amarna family from writing *The Son of the Sun*. It seemed to flow naturally out of its predecessor, my interest in Akhenaten's daughter, Ankhesenpaaten, having been roused by the extraordinary events of her life, and the pressures put upon her as a child.

It could not have been easy to grow up in that family, and she of all her sisters was subjected to events that would have made a modern young girl an instant candidate for the psychiatrist's couch. During her brief life she was married (if only for political reasons!) to her father, her half brother and possibly to her maternal grandfather. That letters have been found from her to the Hittite king asking him to send one of his sons to be King of

Egypt, and are preserved in our archives for anyone to read, gives her added substance.

I have been told that this third of my Egyptian novels is the easiest to read. I wonder if the reason for this is that its gestation occurred with much less interference from outside than the others. When I wrote *Daughter Of Amun* I was somehow trying to accommodate Tina Turner and her belief that she had once been Hatshepsut into the story — though in the end I went my own way. When I wrote *The Son of the Sun* I was constantly under the influence of dreams and mediums and psychic events. But *Daughter of Ra* was more closely based on ordinary research and a strong feeling of sympathy for a child who was subjected to such a life.

It is true a medium told me that Akhenaten, appearing in my living room the week *The Son of the Sun* was first published, said I should write more about his family, and that, as always, I found 'coincidences' coming thick and fast as soon as I started writing.

The book was written faster than the others. I started to research seriously in April 1989 with lectures on the Hittites by George Hart at the British Museum, and study in the library of the Egypt Exploration Society in London.

During this time we were moving house from London to Bath, and we knew that my husband had developed secondary cancers in liver and lungs. Whether it was these stress factors, or because Arrow had not yet finally committed themselves to publishing *The Son of the Sun* so that a sequel was still in question, I don't know, but I was suffering from a major 'writer's block'.

On 5 June I woke at 3 a.m. and suddenly felt the blockage lift. I started writing at once. At 9.30 that same morning I had a phone call from the editor at Arrow saying that they were definitely going to publish *The Son of the Sun* and wanted to see what I had written for the sequel.

I was overjoyed, not least because I felt I had 'picked up' a telepathic message before I had received it by more ordinary means.

During the summer my husband became more and more seriously ill and I had to watch a brilliant, witty man gradually disintegrating under the affects of an inoperable brain tumour.

I hurried with the book because I wanted him to read it before it was too late. He had always been my mentor and critic.

On 6 July my psychic friend, Meryt, saw a vision of

Ankhesenamun handing me a bracelet with a smile. Behind her was a fan bearer. At her side was a small person, child-sized, but dressed in adult clothes. A dwarf? I felt I was on the right track with my writing.

A German friend visited me in London and with her she brought her friend Brigitte. We sat in the crystal and mineral room of the Natural History Museum (a favourite haunt of mine) and talked about Egypt. Brigitte told me how it had come to her (also through a series of extraordinary and uncanny events) that she was a reincarnation of Ankhesenpaaten, who I was now writing about in my book *Daughter of Ra*.

She also told me that she had discovered that all six daughters of Nefertiti were incarnated at this time and all gathered round Berlin where that exquisite and very famous head of Nefertiti is housed in the museum.

If this is true it is most intriguing. I know it is unlikely that all the people who believe they are reincarnations of ancient Egyptian pharaohs can possibly be (I personally have met at least five Akhenatens) but it does seem as though our period is somehow 'twinned' with Eighteenth Dynasty Egypt, powerful emanations from that time and place getting through to us.

Brigitte began to weep as she told me about her experiences as Ankhesenpaaten. She had gone to a place where she habitually went when she wanted to be peaceful and happy, but on this day the atmosphere was shattered. Hostile people with angry faces closed in on her. She was seized and forced to drink poison. She cried out at the injustice of it and kept crying out even after she was dead. Some spirit beings tried to lead her away — but she fought them — still trying to make herself heard.

I listened intently because I had already decided in my own mind before I met Brigitte that Ankhesenpaaten had died by poisoning. It is known she died suddenly and in disgrace for writing to the enemies of Egypt, the Hittites, inviting one of their princes to be her consort. But it is not known how she died.

On 14 September I finished *Daughter of Ra* and submitted it to Arrow.

On 20 September my husband read it, and said it was good. It was the last book he read before he died.

As with all my other books I not only incorporated the academic research I had done, but wove in incidents from my own life. Not long before my husband was too ill to walk we heard that there was to be an eclipse of the moon at 3 a.m. on a certain night. We set the alarm for 2 a.m., wrapped up warmly, and set off, walking, to a little round hill near our home. This hill I am convinced was once a sacred hill used for worship in pagan times, and is still sometimes used for religious purposes at Easter when three crosses are raised on its summit. In my two novels set in Bath, *The Winged Man* and *The Waters of Sul*, this hill features significantly as a gateway between the worlds.

On this night we struggled to the top in the dark and sat down waiting for the eclipse. At 3 a.m. the huge bronze ball of the moon seemed to roll across the sky. In *Daughter of Ra* (chapter 11) I describe a lunar eclipse based on this experience. In the book, Ankhesenamun's experience is tinged with a feeling of dread. As you can imagine, my own experience, knowing that my husband would be dead within weeks of that night, was also tinged with dark emotions — though for different reasons.

As I wrote about Ankhesenamun's fear that she could influence events by her own negative thoughts, I was thinking about my own situation regarding Oliver. We had some New Age friends who insisted he would get better if only I thought positively about his health. I desperately tried to believe he would not die, but he had liver cancer, lung cancer, and a brain tumour and the doctor said he would only live a year, a year ago. Apart from my own suffering watching him disintegrate under my eyes, I now had a terrible gnawing guilt that I was somehow bringing about his death by not believing that he would get well. I did meditations visualizing him in the Cape swimming vigorously in the sea he swam in as a child — but always, always they ended in the darkening shadow of the medical probabilities. No matter how I longed and yearned for him to get better, no matter how I visualised him well, he seemed to get worse day by day. For all my belief in mind and body, spirit and soul, I felt I was failing him by my despair.

From *Tutankhamun and the Daughter of Ra* (chapter 11):

> She looked up to the heavens in her excitement and was shocked to see a dark shadow crossing the face of the moon. At first she thought it must be a cloud but then realised the stars were shining undimmed. It was only the moon that was affected. And then the same cold hand that was grip-

ping the moon seemed to grip her own heart. The thoughts she had been thinking had been dark. She had rejoiced at the destruction of everyone she knew. She had visualized a horrible death for them. What if it was the shadow of her own thoughts that was staining the purity and splendour of the moon?

No one else seemed to see the shadow and she watched as it grew larger and larger, inexorably creeping across the whole face of the moon. Her throat was constricted — dry. She tried to take a sip of wine — but almost choked on it. What if everything she had ever known could be snuffed out? What if it were possible for one's own thoughts to do this? What if one was capable of destroying the universe with nothing more than the intensity of one's thoughts? She knew that one could make oneself ill and heal oneself by thought. She knew also that by projecting malevolent thoughts on to someone else one could make them ill, just as one could lift their spirits and make them well by the intensity of one's benevolent thoughts. Mind could affect mind — there was no doubt about that — and magicians had shown that in certain circumstances material objects could be moved and altered by the mind. But — something as huge and remote as the moon…? The weight of such a responsibility almost crushed her.

In chapter 12 I describe Ankhesenamun's fear of the obsessive, fanatical love of the crowds pressing in around her. That understanding was based on my own experience when in 1988 I travelled to Egypt with Tina Turner and witnessed the almost insane obsession of her fans, and her own fear of being cornered and pulled apart by them.
Tutankhamun and the Daughter of Ra (chapter 12):

This was Ankhesenamun's third marriage. The first had been when she was very young. She had stared at the throngs of excited and admiring people, startled and afraid of their overwhelming, obsessive love. Their faces as they pushed and struggled and strained to get a glimpse of her had struck her as almost insane. What were they hoping to achieve by seeing her? Did they think they could drink her in with their eyes and absorb her into their bodies? The night of that first wedding had passed in restless nightmare. She felt herself backed against the huge wall of the Temple with the crowds pressing and pressing towards her — their mouths open — their eyes staring — their hands reaching out to tear pieces off her... Her father-husband had been kind and comforting when she had woken screaming — and had quietly talked her into the dawn so that she would not have to dream about them again.

Diary entry, 29 March 1987:

Yesterday I bought a green fluorite egg from a crystal stall at the "Prediction Festival", Battersea Town Hall.

I saw it when Oliver and I went on Friday night and I resisted buying it — but couldn't get it out of my mind overnight. I had a real uncontrollable desire for it. So next day, Saturday 28th, I went back to the Festival for no other reason but to get the egg. There was a storm and the weather was really bad. Oliver said he'd give me a lift there but I'd have to make my own way back — which meant a long walk in the rain and cold and a bus ride. I told myself it was crazy. It cost too much and I had a lot of crystals anyway and I was tired and the weather was bad. But, I *had* to go.

I met the man selling the egg and told him I had to have it. He gave me leaflets on his work with crystal healing, and I gave him a leaflet on my books. He said at once he had read my "Tall Stones" trilogy and liked it very much. He noticed on my list I'd written a book about Akhenaten and said he was a medium and was in direct touch with Akhenaten — who called himself 'The Aten' when he came through. I said 'Oh', but didn't really take much notice because a lot of mediums claim a lot of things and not all of them are genuine. I was just intent on buying the egg.

This morning when I woke I suddenly realised he claimed Akhenaten was speaking through him regularly and often, and his name on the leaflet was Manan. This is a name he has chosen. Not the name given to him by his family.

Ma-nan is the name I gave the priest of Amun who controlled the boy oracle in *The Son of the Sun*, and who treated him with such cruelty, and yet, at the end, began to regret what he had done.

Another 'coincidence' connected with the green egg is that last week I handed in my *Women in Celtic Myth* book to the publisher and decided now at last I could get back to the assignment "Akhenaten" had set me through the medium Winifred Franklin — to write two more Egyptian books. I had been delaying the start, making excuses. "He" had been silent all those six months while I'd been caught up in my other commitments — but surfaced again now to remind me (like Hamlet's father's ghost) to get on with the books I had virtually promised him I'd write.

I'd heard about "the green stone" from Andrew Collins, a writer I'd met at one of the festivals for 'Mind, Body and Spirit' in London, and then read the book *The Green Stone* by Graham Philips and Martin Keatman (published by Panther, 1984) which is the extraordinary story of their search for a green stone that was once supposed to have belonged to Akhenaten and which they were 'told' to find. In the search they were driven by psychic forces that eventually got the upper hand.

In chapter 4 of *Tutankhamun and the Daughter of Ra*, I have based the idea of the Sacred Egg of Ra not only on all the references in ancient Egyptian to the Cosmic Egg out of which the universe is hatched, but on my own collection of crystal eggs. Whether my own fascination with crystal eggs came before I read the Egyptian texts, or after, I am not sure. All my life I have been interested in ancient Egypt. All my life I have collected crystals and noticed their power on the emotions and the imagination.

The reader has probably noticed that certain parts of all my books have mythic truth and certain parts have literal truth — as near as we can get it after more than three thousand years. The green Egg of Ra belongs to the realm of myth. In ancient Egyptian myth one of the central ideas is that of a Sacred Egg out of which all that exists is hatched. Therefore, I have used the Sacred Egg in this story as a major theme, not because Ankhesenamun and the others literally struggled for possession of an actual crystal egg, although it may well have happened more or less as I describe, but because, like our western European myth about the Holy Grail, it serves to illustrate certain important aspects of the characters involved and, by analogy, the human race. Each pursued it for a different reason and, like the Holy Grail, it was not only different things to different people, but sometimes different things to the same person.

In Chapter 11 of *Daughter of Ra*, Ankhesenamun's pain at the death of Tutankhamun is based on my own pain at the imminent loss of my husband:

> Chanting spells from the ancient Book of the Great Awakening, the deceased King in his heavy and unwieldy mummiform nest of coffins was lowered carefully down the steep steps to the tomb itself. Ankhesenamun suddenly cried out and almost fell as she rushed forward to hold him once more in her arms. The dust that she had flung over herself in the traditional way as she walked on her white sandaled feet to the Valley of the Kings, showered over the gold and turquoise, the lapis lazuli and carnelian.
>
> 'O Lord of Flame,' she whispered, 'who guards the two eyes of the sky — who opens the two eyes of the sky — bind me a ladder. Make me a way that I may follow the love of my heart. I am weary of the Heh Gods, of the Watery Abyss, of the Disappearing One, of the Darkness!'
>
> […]
>
> I am thy wife, O great one – do not leave me!
>
> Is it thy good pleasure, O my brother, that I should go far from thee?
>
> How can it be that I go away alone?
>
> I say: I accompany thee, O thou who didst like to converse with me, but thou remainest silent and speakest not!

We had talked a lot, Oliver and I. He used words brilliantly, witty and colourful. One of the saddest things to watch as his brain tumour took over, was the loss of his ability to speak.

On 23 June 1987, I had a strange experience at George Hart's lecture on "Akhenaten to Ay".

Looking at the slide of Tutankhamun as an infant head rising from a lotus — suddenly I felt "strange" and that the head was no longer a piece of sculpture but a face of flesh and blood — the eyes looking directly at me and the lips beginning to move to say something. Startled, I stared — but instantly Hart changed the slide and it was gone. I was left dazed, frustrated, wondering what he was trying to say.

My sister Joan had had a similar experience the second my mother died. Thousands of miles away and unaware of my mother's death she suddenly saw the disembodied head of my mother hovering near her — mouth moving — trying to speak — but no voice coming out. It faded almost instantly.

After my experience at the lecture, I was working on the story of Tutankhamun. At six o'clock in the evening I went downstairs to start preparing Oliver's dinner. I switched on the television. It was the BBC news and they were talking about Tutankhamun. Boxes full of seeds and flowers that were put in Tutankhamun's tomb with him had been re-discovered in a forgotten cupboard at Kew Gardens where they had lain for fifty years. It gave me such a strange feeling. The boy I was writing about, that I was trying to bring to life again in my writing, the boy who had lived more than 3000 years ago, was being spoken about on the contemporary news with all the contemporary bits and pieces as though his death and burial were part of our lives today. It is always a pleasant surprise when something as exoteric as the news service gives proof of an esoteric truth.

IV: *The Ghost of Akhenaten*

When The Son of the Sun *was published I received so many letters from people around the world claiming to have a personal connection with Akhenaten, either by reincarnation, or by dreams, or channelling, that I began to realise that Akhenaten was still a player in the world today.*

But even without these personal connections, Akhenaten has always been one of our best known pharaohs from ancient Egypt, either because he is supposed to be the first monotheist in the ancient world, or because of his relationship to Tutankhamun whose tomb was found in the 1920s and whose treasures have become familiar to us in museums, and in films and books. Perhaps another reason we are so fascinated by him is that after his death in mysterious circumstances, information about him was suppressed. His successors tried to wipe the memory of him from history. Our curiosity is always aroused when we suspect someone is trying to keep something from us.

Archaeologists in the nineteenth century began to uncover intriguing hints and clues about the existence of a "heretic pharaoh" in the Eighteenth Dynasty, and began to excavate the ruins of his dream city in Middle Egypt at Amarna.

In The Ghost of Akhenaten *I describe a modern group, based in Bath, who travel to lay the ghost of Akhenaten which is reported to have been seen in Egypt, and to free him from the spell that they believe his enemies, the priests of Amun, put on him.*

At a time when contemporary religious factions in the world are killing each other daily, the violent struggle between the followers of Amun and the Aten delivers a disturbing message about the human race.

We moved from London to Bath in Somerset early in 1989. My husband Oliver died of cancer on 14 November 1989.

The last manuscript of mine he read was *Daughter of Ra*, which was published by Arrow in 1990. After he died I wrote *Myths of the Sacred Tree*, *The Winged Man*, and *The Waters of Sul*.

The Egyptian trilogy was out of print in English, but in print in Germany. In 1997 Neue Erde published a booklet on the writing of *Son of the Sun* "My Encounter with Akhenaten". I received many letters from German readers — more than one claiming to be a reincarnation of Akhenaten, and some reporting on their own encounters with Akhenaten.

It seemed to me that Akhenaten was very much "alive" in the consciousness of the present age.

Without consciously intending to, I found myself incubating another book about Akhenaten.

Several threads came together. One, and perhaps the most powerful, was that I felt dissatisfied that I had not yet resolved the matter of Akhenaten's "after death" relationship with the Priests of Amun. I had rejected D.K.'s suggestion of going to Egypt in 1994 to lift the curse personally. But what if I travelled to Egypt on the "astral plane", or somehow psychically, and attempted to lift it this way? After all, it was taking place on another level of reality than the material anyway. By 1998 when I had this idea I was so crippled with arthritis that I could not have travelled physically to Egypt. I had lost touch with D.K. For a few years after our meeting in 1994 I had received postcards from him from around the world every few months telling me about his attempts to raise the money to get a film made of *The Son of the Sun*, plus a new publication of it. He was also trying to raise money for our journey to Egypt to lift the curse — which in itself would be part of the film project.

But even these cards had ceased to come and we had lost contact completely.

The second thread that was weaving in and out of my mind at this time concerned my feelings about "the New Age". In 1976 when my "Tall Stones" novels had been written and were starting to be published, the "New Age" was a new concept to me. I remember finding the first festival of "Mind and Body" at Olympia in London so exciting because it seemed that long disregarded spiritual ideas were bubbling to the surface, and many people were looking for an alternative to the materialism of society.

My books were taken up enthusiastically by the New Age and at the festivals of "Mind, Body and Spirit" that proliferated at that time, my books were being sold in great numbers. I was receiving letters from all over the world about how *The Tall Stones* and its series was changing the consciousness of the readers, and helping them spiritually.

But over the years these festivals became more and more commercial. From the early days when it represented a revolution in thinking, it went the same way as most mass movements — people who didn't really understand the profundity of the wisdom that lay behind it, jumped on the bandwagon to cash in on the commercial possibilities.

My publisher, Arrow, asked me to write a book about healing with crystals not because they believed in it, but because other publishers were making a lot of money publishing books about it. I had read several of these books. Most of them were superficial. Most of them derivative of each other. I refused, but said I would like to write a book about the myths and legends about crystals that would show why we *expected* crystals to heal us. Arrow refused. They wanted a book the same as all the others. I did write my book, *Crystal Legends*, but it took an enterprising editor at Arkana to take it on.

In 1976 when I was healed of angina by a spirit healer in Bristol, he would take no money, because he said it was Spirit who healed me. He was only the conduit.

In later years healers of many types sprung up, some after only a week's course in their particular discipline. They charged a lot. Some were genuine. Some were false.

I began to worry that the genuine insights of the New Age would be lost if a backlash set in against the gullible and the fake.

I wanted to write a book exposing the bad elements in the New Age movement, while attempting to promote the good elements.

In *The Ghost of Akhenaten* I describe Glastonbury, a famous New Age centre near my home town of Bath.

From *The Ghost of Akhenaten* (chapter 2):

> Emma always felt she was entering a special realm when she entered Glastonbury. Not only did it resonate with its extraordinary history, but also the contemporary scene itself was like nowhere else she had ever encountered.

Eliot was cynical about Glastonbury. He claimed that it was all sham and fake. He hated the vegetarian cafes, the shops that sold crystals at exorbitant prices just because they were supposed to be impregnated with healing energies. He hated the women who had substituted one gender of an impossible god for another, and the statues of gross fat women purporting to be images of the Earth Goddess. But most of all he hated the ragged unemployed who hung about the streets like hippies left over from the sixties, with matted hair, ear-rings and dogs on leads of frayed string.

Emma saw it as an exciting mix of many different cultures. The farmers used it as a market town. The Christians earnestly paraded through the streets with crosses and candles on certain days of the church calendar. Then there were the New Agers who built invisible temples and walked an invisible maze on the Tor, who had rituals they believed dated back to ancient times. Shops sold Christian icons beside images of pagan gods and goddesses, magnificent reproductions of Medieval and Renaissance archangels beside impossibly fey paintings of tree devas and angels looking like winged Barbie dolls. And on every notice board were advertisements promising alternative and complementary healing.

Emma believed that there were genuine seekers after enlightenment there, and inexplicable miracles of healing. She claimed that for every charlatan overcharging for bogus alternative healing there was one who was truly in touch with the spiritual dimension that brings wholeness to the fractured psyche. She believed that tucked away among the bookshelves in shops and libraries housing so many superficial panaceas for the ills of the world, there were genuine gems of wisdom that could change your life for the better and divert the world from destruction.

In this same chapter I described a version of "past life readings" I myself had, and expressed my own dissatisfaction with them in Jack's dissatisfaction with Denise at Glastonbury.

One of the things I wanted to explore in *The Ghost of Akhenaten* is the ambiguity and confusion of channelling and psychic experiences.

Surrounded by portraits of her spirit guides; wispy Tibetans, stern ancient Egyptians and one magnificent Amerindian in full feathered head-dress; he was offered herbal tea, and sat, sipping it out of a bone china cup, as Emma and Denise talked.

Emma had promised she would not tell Denise any details about his dreams, but just that he needed a past life reading to see if they had any relevance to his present life. He wanted to see what she could pick up psychically.

He soon felt uneasy under the stare of the disembodied beings she believed communicated with her. Emma and Mary seemed to be unperturbed by the belief that they were surrounded by invisible beings of various species and orders — some the dead who chose to return to try to help the living, others who had never lived on earth yet interacted with it in a dynamic way... Had not Abraham been visited by angels, and Paul heard voices on the road to Damascus? But what if Denise's voices were mischievous or ignorant? Enlightenment might not come as an automatic result of dying, but have to be won by passing further trials and tests in the Afterlife.

Yet another theme I wanted to express in the book was the universality of religious intolerance. Akhenaten had overthrown the traditional gods of his people and set up the Aten as the sole god of Egypt channelled through him and his family. When he died — and he may well have been assassinated for his beliefs — the pharaohs that came after him, Ay, Tutankhamun and Horemheb, made sure the old gods were reinstated and Akhenaten himself declared a heretic and all that he stood for declared anathema. This all happened more than 3000 years ago and yet *still* religious fundamentalists are killing each other in the names of their gods.

From *The Ghost of Akhenaten* (chapter 18):

How long they were trapped in that small space while the dark forces of the storm tore at the fabric of their vehicle, they could not tell, but at last the noise subsided and they ventured to pull the covers down from the windows and look out. Sand had found its way into the jeep through tiny cracks and Emma's face was streaked where the tears had run down through it.

Thankfully they opened the windows and forced the doors against the sand that had piled up around them, and took great gulps of fresh air. The sky was blood red.

And then they stumbled out and looked around.

The landscape had completely changed. Sand had covered many of the rocks that had been visible before, and exposed others that had not. But strangest of all strange sights were the skeletons of military tanks and guns now lying before them.

They looked to Hassan for an explanation.

'They must have been left behind after the war,' he said. 'They were buried under the sand.'

'Just under the surface,' Jack thought, 'the ghosts of religious wars.' How many other wars lay covered — biding their time to resurface?

But what was uppermost in my mind when I chose to write this further book about Akhenaten was that I wanted to make sense of all the strange experiences I had had in connection with the writing of *The Son of the Sun*. I was particularly interested in the fact that I had received so many letters from people who claimed to be the reincarnation of Akhenaten. Surely they all could not be? What was going on?

In early 1999 I finished the novel and sent it to my son Strat to read. I had incorporated myself and my own experiences during the writing of *The Son of the Sun* into it, branching out halfway into the adventurers of a group of fictional characters who go to Egypt, on my suggestion, to seek out *The Ghost of Akhenaten* and lift the curse. But Strat said the book would confuse the readers with this mixture of autobiography and fantasy, so I rewrote it, leaving out all the overtly autobiographical material and making the whole thing fictional. But — as Lord Lytton said about his novel *Zanoni* in 1853 — "It is a romance, and it is not a romance. It is a book for those who comprehend it, and an extravagance for those who cannot."

I have always thought my books, often marketed as "Fantasy Fiction" because bookshops insist on categories, are anything but "fantasy". They are truth for those who comprehend them, and an extravagance for those who do not.

In the second version of the book there was still a Mary Brown, an old woman with arthritis like myself, who had an interest in Akhenaten and believed he had been cursed, but I gave her a different set of experiences to my own. It was no longer strictly autobiographical but, as all authors do, many of the incidents described had actually happened to me, though they were now fictionalized for the purposes of the story.

For instance, the incident in the market in Cairo where Emma gets pulled into a shop and kissed by a strange man, happened to me in 1982. In reality I was not rescued by a mysterious man in a dove grey suit, but by my travelling companions.

Another instance of a personal experience used in the story is the exorcism scene in the Monastery of the Virgin near Amarna. This was witnessed by me in 1982 — but my experience was in a coptic church in Cairo.

From *The Ghost of Akhenaten* (chapter 9):

> The four westerners were silent. This primitive and macabre ceremony was performed in the holy of holies of a Christian church. Was what they intended to do — to rescue a ghost from a three thousand year old curse — so very different? Jack thought about the exorcisms he had heard about in England. There were no chains and no mumbo jumbo, no dark and furtive ceremonies, but a belief, nonetheless, that dark spirits *did* exist, and *could* take over the living. For the first time he felt truly afraid of what they were doing. Up to now it had seemed an adventure, almost a game. He realised that he had not seriously believed there was a real ghost, a real curse, and a real dark force they would have to confront. Belief comes in stages like the steps they had just climbed. At first you think you believe something — but don't really. The next stage is when you think you believe in something, and start to act upon it as though it is real. You play out the moves that are expected of you if what you believe is true. But your deepest consciousness is not engaged. But then suddenly something shakes you into really believing! And this stage is different from all that have gone before.
>
> He looked at the others. Bernard was looking ill at ease. Finn's face he could not see but Emma was plainly terrified. She too had met herself face to face in that dark place.

Just as the stones of Akhenaten's city Akhetaten were taken

on his demise to build the city of Hermopolis across the Nile, and other structures north and south of the deserted ruin, I have taken my own experiences out of context and have used them to give texture and verity to the structure of the novel I have written.

The idea that someone could be cursed at death so that he would not be able to journey through the realms of the Afterlife, but would be pinned to the earth in some way, came to me in the stone circle at Arbor Low, Derbyshire in July 1979. I wrote this experience into the first chapter of my novel *The Tower and the Emerald*, and later I learned that such curses were known from ancient Egypt.

The Ghost of Akhenaten starts with such a curse.

From *The Ghost of Akhenaten* (chapter 1):

The man lay on the desert sand, his body twisted and broken.

Dark shapes circled around him like jackals around a lion's kill.

Deep voices intoned the malevolent words of a curse.

'This man will not rise again.
This man will not go to the stars.
This man will lie forever in the desert cut off from those who loved him and those whom he loved.
His god will have no access to him.
HIS GOD IS DEAD.'

The sky deepened from the colour of fire to the colour of blood.

One broke off from the circle, crouched and wrote hieroglyphs in the sand — each one reversed.

The chanting continued.

'May you never enter the barque that glides among the unwearying stars. May you forget the names of those who guard the seven doors, the fourteen gates, the twenty-one mounds of the Otherworld, and may you never be vindicated in the presence of the forty-two assessors. May your heart weigh heavy against the feather of Maat in the Hall of Osiris, and Ammut, the Devourer of the Dead, feed on it. You have

denied the gods of your ancestors, may they in the Everlasting deny you.'

Darkness fell and absorbed the figures of the priests who changed these fearsome words, as though they were part of the darkness itself.

When the dawn came and the sun rose in a splendour of blue and gold, the man who lay, twisted and broken, alone at the centre of a vast and featureless desert, did not witness it.

I received a sort of confirmation in 1994 that I had been right to think the Priests of Amun had cursed Akhenaten to pin him to the earth. I met D.K., who told me he had met a Bedouin who had met the ghost of Akhenaten in the desert, claiming to have been cursed by the Priests of Amun. The Bedouin had not read my book *The Son of the Sun*. D.K. got in touch with me when he found *The Son of the Sun* in a second hand bookshop, read it and remembered what the Bedouin had told him.

In the new version of *The Ghost of Akhenaten* I gave Mary Brown a different reason than my own for believing in the curse, though I do bring in the Bedouin's experience.

From *The Ghost of Akhenaten* (chapter 5):

'The book *Tombs, Temples and Ancient Art* by Joseph Lindon Smith, edited by his wife Corinna, described a weird event. Lindon Smith was an artist who accompanied archaeologists in Egypt to record their findings. In 1909 he and Arthur Weigall decided to put on a play about Akhenaten in the Valley of the Queens. The idea behind it was that the Priests of Amun had cursed Akhenaten so that in death he would not be able to travel to the Otherworld, but would be doomed to walk the earth forever as a powerless ghost. The play intended to lift the curse and free the soul to travel on.

'In January 1909 several archaeologists and their families and friends gathered in the Valley at Luxor to watch the dress rehearsal. Arthur Weigall and Joseph Lindon Smith had written the text between them and they and their wives were taking the major roles.

'After the invocation Hortense as "Akhenaten" appeared on a crag above the stage. As the actress raised her arms in supplication to the god a devastating peal of thunder and a blinding flash of lightening struck. A wind sprang up as if from nowhere and rushed screaming through the narrow valley. Lindon Smith described how they clutched their possessions at once and bent double against the blast. The donkeys, which had brought them to the valley, set up a terrified braying.

'But almost as suddenly as it had started the storm was over, and they decided to continue the rehearsal, laughing at the dramatic interruption, and joking about the Priests of Amun trying to intimidate them.

'The rehearsal continued, but again, later, when Queen Tiye was declaiming Akhenaten's Hymn to the Aten and making an impassioned plea, for his release, another violent storm swept through the valley, this time with squalls of rain and hail stones as big as tennis balls. Most of them fled at this point to the shelter of a tomb, but Corinna in her persona as Queen Tiye, stood dramatically and firmly on her rock and continued her recital of the long hymn to its very end. When her husband drew her away she was soaked to the skin, but wild with excitement that she had defied the elements and the ancient Priests of Amun.

'It was impossible to continue this time, and they retreated to the tombs for shelter. That night they slept uneasily.

'In the morning it emerged that both Corinna and Hortense had had an identical dream in which one of the statues in the Ramesseum had come alive and whipped her with his flail, Corinna in the eyes, and Hortense in the stomach. Both women were in great pain in the part of the body where they had been hit in the dream. Later Corinna had to be rushed to a Cairo hospital with a dangerous case of trachoma. Most of those who had been at the rehearsal were ill. The play was abandoned.'

When Mary finished speaking there was silence for a while in the room.

Emma shuddered. 'The dark forces are very real and we challenge them at our peril!' she said.

'Do you believe there really is a ghost and a curse?' Jack asked Mary.

She shrugged. 'My persistent dreams make sense if there

is,' she replied. 'And then, just as the time I was really pondering the truth about all this, I met a man who claimed to have seen Akhenaten's ghost in the desert in Egypt. He claimed that Akhenaten himself told him he had been cursed, and pleaded with him to try and release him. I felt I could no longer ignore the possibility that it might be true, and began to wonder what I could do about it. Archaeologists and Egyptologists don't know what happened to Akhenaten in the end. His successors did everything in their power to eliminate all record of him from history. Something sinister must have gone on!'

This play of Weigall and Lindon Smith and what happened in 1909 is a genuine historical fact. I read about it first on 11 August 1986, *after* I had written *The Son of the Sun*.

My belief that Mary Brown could travel with them to Egypt using telepathy and dream, is based on my own experience. I have had many potent and meaningful dreams, and many cases of telepathy. I have even had an extraordinary experience of bi-location — in 1976 when I was inspired to write thirty-five poems about the power of the Christ/Fish symbol I had apparently appeared to a woman and talked her out of suicide.

My attitude to channellers has always been ambivalent. I believe disembodied people can use a living person in order to communicate, but I believe also it is very easy to fake. The channeller could quite easily be projecting fake voices to influence and manipulate events to demonstrate his or her power over others, or he or she might sincerely believe they are providing a channel for communication from the other world, but are deceiving themselves. But even if, in some cases, there is a genuine case of channelling, it should still be treated with great caution. When I am asked whether my books are channelled I say "No". They may be "inspired" by help from other worlds, or from my own higher consciousness, but I don't believe I have given up my autonomy to be "taken over" by another. I am open to suggestions or advice from living or dead friends, but it is my decision whether to act on the suggestions or not, and if I do, it will be within my own field of understanding and experience.

Another incident from my own life that influenced something I wrote into the book *The Ghost of Akhenaten* was the mummified hand from ancient Egypt I once possessed. My husband and I visited someone once, many years ago in the 1960s, and were shown a shrivelled mummified hand from ancient Egypt. I remember it was thin and delicate like a young woman's hand with well-shaped nails painted with red henna. The husband of the house said his wife hated it and felt it was haunting them in some way, and longed to get rid of it. Oliver said at once that we would take it away if they wanted us to. He stressed that I was particularly interested in ancient Egypt. We set off for home on the London underground tube train, me holding the hand in a paper bag on my lap, feeling really pleased with my new acquisition. I remember smiling to myself thinking that the people sitting next to me on the train had no idea what a macabre object was in the paper bag.

But within days of having it in my home I also began to feel uneasy about it. I felt it was haunting the house and longed to get rid of it. But one couldn't just throw such an historic and valuable object into the trash bin. I seem to remember (though I have to check this) that my son Julian swapped it for an air rifle at school — or did he sell it to a neighbour's child? Either way it was passed on and I never saw it again.

But the feelings I had when it was in the house were what I drew on for Jack's feelings about the Tomb Guard in his apartment, and Jack's dream about the stone hand beckoning in his dream. The stone hand was based on an amalgam of my own possession of the mummified hand and the plaster facsimile of Akhenaten's hand on the wall in my friend Meryt's house in London.

Diary entry, 23 November 1988:

Made uneasy by a phone call from someone claiming to be a reincarnation of Akhenaten. He says I met and spoke to him at one of those New Age Festivals a year ago. He expected me to remember him although he hadn't given me his name — and still didn't. He says he has now read my *Son of the Sun* and the battle between Akhenaten and the dark priests of Amun is still going on, and he is caught up in it. He says he's going to Egypt for the first time "in this life" in December and knows that there will be a dangerous confrontation then. So he wanted to meet me to talk about what I knew so that he would go into the battle

fully armed. What I wrote in my book was not fiction he said —
but really did happen and was still happening.

I said I did not want to meet him because I did not want to
get more involved than I already was. I was prepared to write
my books — but I wanted to do that by myself and in my own
way. I didn't want to get involved in *his* battle and do it *his* way.
He was persistent, but I was adamant. I'm finally learning how
to resist being 'taken over' by people. When I wrote *Son of the
Sun* it was T. This time — I want to steer clear of forceful people
trying to influence me to write *their* book — if I can.

On my second visit to Egypt I experienced the suddenness and
devastation of a sandstorm which I describe in chapter 18 of
The Ghost of Akhenaten. I was not personally in a ramshackle
jeep at the time, but in a tourist shop. The ramshackle jeep experience
occurred to me in Jordan in 1993 in the Waddi Rhum.

Emma's feelings as she entered the tomb of Horemheb in
chapter 17 of *The Ghost of Akhenaten* were my own feelings as I
entered his tomb in 1982 having just completed *The Son of the
Sun* — believing that Horemheb had been one of Akhenaten's
most dangerous enemies, and that I was somehow on the side
of Akhenaten.

The gunshots Emma and Jack heard in the Valley of the
Kings I had heard in 1988. Again it was I who was told by a
tomb guide that it was a Japanese film company, and I who had
mused on the different levels of reality and illusion in everyday
life.

Mary Brown's fascination with the statue of Akhenaten in the
Louvre was based on my own fascination during my visit to
Paris in early March 1982.

Emma's strange dream about the Book of Thoth in chapter
15 of *The Ghost of Akhenaten* is based on one of my own
dreams and the fact that I have found the ancient Egyptian
story about that mysterious and powerful book a constant
source of inspiration.

In my book *Crystal Legends* I told the whole story and my
own interpretation of it.

The Book of Thoth — a kind of ancient Egyptian Holy Grail
or Ark of the Covenant that destroys the unauthorized who
touch it but gives great rewards to those for whom it is meant —
has been the subject of much speculation. Some suggest that

the Tarot pack is all that is left to us of it — picture cards containing images that hold the Mysteries in secret hibernation, like a cave holds a bear in winter. Come the spring of our enlightenment, the images wake, and we know 'the essence and power of all things' (Psellus, a Byzantine philosopher quoted on p.19 of Frederic Lionel's book *The Magic Tarot*).

Some link it to the 'Emerald Tablet' of the alchemists, containing instructions for transforming one thing into another on the grounds that, differing only in scale, all things, from the cosmos to the atom, are governed by the same intrinsic laws.

Both Ne-nefer-ka-Ptah and Khaemwaset are informed by old and dying men where the book may be found but warned about the dangers of trying to acquire it. It is as though it is not intended that the secret whereabouts of the book should be totally lost, yet knowledge of its hiding place should be kept by a line of initiates throughout the centuries, only to be revealed on death to the next in line.

Almost all cultures have a myth in which some knowledge is felt to be so powerful, so dangerous if held by the wrong person, that it must be kept secret and only released after the most stringent and rigorous of testing to the care of the chosen guardian. This concept might have sprung from our own bewilderment at being faced by the extraordinary mystery of existence. We know we are here, but we don't know why, or how we came to be here in the first place. We don't know if there is someone in control who has a purpose and a design for us — or if our lives are pointless, rudderless, and random. We can believe — but we cannot know for sure. Because we fear that knowing everything may well spoil the adventure of living and remove all incentive to explore and progress, and yet we fear that if there is never any chance of knowing we will despair equally and give up trying, we like to posit that the knowledge is accessible only to a select and superior few, who will guard it and keep it safely 'in trust' for us. But even this has its dangers — even honoured and dependable people can prove to be as fallible as the rest of us. There is the danger that the knowledge we desire and yet fear might be misused and somehow we, or the world we know, might be destroyed. I think that is why there are so many myths like the above, stressing the danger of the Secret and the need for careful and honourable guardianship.

The Curse. Someone once asked me if curses really worked and I was hesitant in my reply. I still don't know for sure — but I think I tend to believe in them though I wish I didn't. I know certainly they work if you believe in them. African witch doctors and Haitian voodoo practitioners know this and there are many documented cases of people dying because they *believed* they were dying having been cursed by a witch doctor. The mind is extraordinary powerful and no one completely understands its mechanism of belief. There are faith healings as well as faith killings, and people recover from fatal illnesses many times when there is no more explanation then that they believed they would get well. Faith can have a physical effect. Fear releases certain harmful chemicals into the body as does despair and anxiety. Other helpful chemicals might be released by joyful conviction and positive thinking. Even if you believe in nothing but matter, and dismiss the existence of soul and spirit, there is physical evidence to explain these things.

We all know about the extraordinary feats Hindu Sadhus can perform — walking on fire, passing metal spikes through their bodies, sleeping on nails, etc.

When I was eighteen two friends and I dabbled with an Ouija board. One friend was told she would die at twenty-seven, and I would die at thirty-five. She did die at twenty-seven — of flu. Did she die because she believed she would die? At thirty-five I was nervous, but I was married to a very sensible, rational man, and my beliefs in such things were no longer as strong. I did not die. I wrote this into *The Ghost of Akhenaten* as happening to Finn. This was not strictly a curse. I quote it only because it is an incident from my own experience where I think the belief in the inevitability of death may have played a part in my friend's death.

I have also read in my father's family history that one of his brothers was killed by a witch doctor — though I don't know the details. My father's family were "god fearing" Christian pioneers who had emigrated from England to settle on a remote farm in Natal, South Africa, in 1880. This incident occurred not long after their arrival.

Whether a curse such as the one believed to have been laid on Akhenaten by the priests of Amun over 3000 years ago could still be operating or not, is a difficult question to answer. And I cannot answer it.

I write fiction, but fiction has to be believable or it will not grip the reader. Fiction is woven out of an author's own experiences, imagination and speculations based on the observation of other peoples lives.

I know for instance that the ancient Egyptians believed in curses and there are many, many texts about them. The media whipped up enthusiasm for ancient Egyptians curses when Carter opened the tomb of Tutankhamun in the 1922. Certainly many things happened that could have been attributed to a curse — but many other things attributed to it could be explained away. That Lord Carnarvon, who had financed the excavation, died so suddenly so soon afterwards of a septic mosquito bite was alarming, but Carter himself lived many years afterwards.

Another factor that makes me hesitantly believe in curses is the power of another person's thoughts. Not only does telepathy exist, for me, incontrovertibly — but we all know how strong personalities can influence us to act in ways we might not normally. We all know how sometimes a house "feels" dark and malevolent and then we find out later that a horrific murder took place there. Another house feels light and comforting because the people who lived there were happy. It is as though thought form projected by powerful emotion *can* hang about in the air.

Within the context of Akhenaten's life the curse is believable. Within the context of ancient Egyptian religion, it is believable. In the context of the twenty-first century, so little is known still about the mind and the forces at play in the universe — even the physical forces — that the feasibility of such a curse cannot be dismissed outright.

In chapter 18 of *The Ghost of Akhenaten*, Eliot, who may have been a reincarnation of one of the priests of Amun who had originally cursed Akhenaten, is confronted by the consequences of a curse on the one who curses:

Eternal Life? The English Eliot had not thought he believed in it, and until this moment, in this desolate and haunted place, he had not thought he needed to believe in it. But what if one was accountable for one's actions — and not only in this life? What if there was a series of realms through which one had to progress, watched and tested all the time?

What if he had lived before and committed unspeakable deeds for which he would have to pay? What if — and the thought would not go away — what if *he* was the one who had cursed Akhenaten and was himself locked, like him, in the savagery of that curse forever. Mary had said a curse binds him who is cursed and him who curses.

When I came to write *The Ghost of Akhenaten* I did not consult my previous novel about Akhenaten, *The Son of the Sun*, in every detail. I didn't even read it through again, though it was ten years since I had last read it. The thought that Akhenaten had been assassinated and cursed by the Priests of Amun was constant, but the two books did not mesh in every way. However, I have just re-read the pages in *The Son of the Sun* where Djehuti-Kheper-Ra and the half reformed priest Ma-nan found the bones of Akhenaten in the desert and attempted to give him a proper burial. This occurred shortly after Akhenaten's death. In *The Ghost of Akhenaten*, more than 3000 years have gone by.

It is not inconceivable that Emma found the same bones Djehuti-Kheper-Ra found and buried, and that she, Jack and Finn performed their own version of the burial. In a sense everything that ever happens, happens over and over again, with variations, each performer learning more from the performance than the last, each performance having its own personal significance for the performer.

Between the writing and publication of the two books I had come to believe that Akhenaten's soul was still pinned to the earth partly because I heard of the play performed in 1909 which had such dire consequences. Also, my own dreams, experiences and intuitions, and the accounts of his ghost being seen in Egypt claiming that he had been cursed by the Priests of Amun, played a part.

The booklet *My Encounter with Akhenaten*, published in 1997 to accompany the German editions of my Egyptian trilogy, contains a description of all the extraordinary things that happened to me while writing *The Son of the Sun* and ended with the following passage:

> This time I believe a way to defeat the Priests of Amun who might, or might not, still be overshadowing these events is to pray, and to ask all who read this to pray, that the Great

One beyond all Other, bearing whatever name in whatever culture, may give release and freedom to the soul of Akhenaten — and at the same time, to release his enemies from their bitter hatred which has, and is, imprisoning them as surely as any spell they may have cast has imprisoned Akhenaten.

It may be that when Djehuti-Kheper-Ra prayed for the release of Akhenaten's soul in the desert (chapter 14, *The Son Of The Sun*) he did not do enough. He should have also prayed for the souls of his enemies that they would relinquish their hate — 'that they would see — and, in seeing, change their ways' (chapter 10). There can be no going forward in peace, no healing, when there is hate and resentment still present. There can be no breaking a spell effectively when the energy that put it in place is left as powerful as it was.

I would ask all who now read this book to join with me in prayer for both the soul of Akhenaten and those who hated him. The words may be your own but let the prayer be from the heart.

'Great God, creator of all the universes and all the different realities within all the universes, who sends servants of light throughout all Time and Space to do Thy Will, to help and guide those struggling… send us forth in Thy Light… without fear and without weakness… Release the soul of Akhenaten and his enemies to progress in light according to Thy Will — that hate will fall away and love will flourish and endure.'

It might be good to pray looking up at the night sky, for the ancient pharaohs believed that when they were freed from the earth they joined the stars…

Whether this is the end of the curse on Akhenaten I do not know. Whether there was ever literally a curse and a ghost I do not know. I have written an adventure story and within it I have woven many of the threads from my own life, travelling, as we all do, through a multi-dimensional universe in multi-dimensional time. That Akhenaten so powerfully stirs the imagination of so many of us 3000 years after his death must mean something.

Seven

Anglo Saxon Britain (Seventh Century)

Etheldreda

Etheldreda, Princess of East Anglia, Queen of Northumbria and Abbess of Ely, was a remarkable woman who lived in restless, violent times not unlike our own, when old beliefs were dying and new ones were struggling to emerge. Pagan clashed with Christian as the seven kingdoms of the Germanic tribes warred against each other and against the native Celts. Occasionally an uneasy peace was bought by the skilful use of the 'diplomatic marriage', and twice Etheldreda, though vowed to chastity, submitted to marriage for political reasons. When her second husband refused to accept the 'arrangement' between them, she fled south, her escape to the Island of Ely apparently aided by storms that intervened on her behalf. She lived only a few years as abbess of the religious community she founded at Ely before dying of plague. Ever since, pilgrims have turned to her for miracles of help and healing.

One evening in June 1978, my husband and I were passing through Ely in Cambridgeshire, five minutes before the famous abbey was about to close. I rushed in to see what I could see in that brief moment and picked up a pamphlet about Saint Etheldreda, the seventh century Anglo Saxon queen who had founded the abbey.

Her life and her times began to fascinate me and I built up quite a dossier of information about her, but somehow I could not see how to write a book about her. Inspiration was lacking.

Some time later we had occasion to return to Cambridgeshire. Oliver was doing the illustrations for a book by Shirley Toulson: *East Anglia: Walking the Ley Lines and Ancient Tracks*.

On a cold dark winter's evening we looked for a hotel for the night. The one recommended to us was shut for the winter. We drove from village to village looking for accommodation and finally settled, exhausted, in a place the name of which we had not noticed. We booked into the hotel at 10pm and went straight to bed. A few days earlier I had decided to abandon my plan to write a novel about Saint Etheldreda as I felt it was too difficult.

At 2am I jerked awake as though someone had hit me in the chest. Startled, I lay awake, wondering if the hotel was haunted. I could feel a Presence in the room. Strangely I was not afraid — but interested. And then I found that the whole story of Etheldreda came vividly alive for me. I was wide awake and very excited. I knew exactly how to write the book and, indeed, that I *had* to write it.

In the morning we discovered that we were at East Dereham, and the hotel was built on the site of the shrine of Saint Etheldreda's sister, Saint Withberga. Her body had lain there for centuries, visited by thousands of pilgrims.

Now the writing flowed easily, and as it did, I thought a great deal about my own Christian beliefs. In my exploration of religions throughout the world I neglected Christianity, partly because I believed it was so familiar to me that I need not bother, and partly because I feared commitment to any one religion — all of them having something to give me, and none of them enough.

During the writing of *Etheldreda* I realised the familiarity I felt with Christianity was only superficial. The memory of the powerful experience at my confirmation in 1940, when I felt the inrush of the Holy Spirit as the Bishop's hands touched my head, had faded, and I reverted to mouthing biblical and liturgical passages like many church-goers, without a conscious awareness of their meaning. Through Etheldreda's passionate commitment to Christ I began to wake up to the real meaning behind the familiar words.

Looking back on that time I can remember the effort, the struggle to come to terms with something I had rejected when I married my agnostic husband, Oliver. Another thread in the weave of my complex emotions at this time was my relationship with one of my sisters, Rhona. She and her husband had been 'born again' and were now closely associated with a strong evangelical branch of Christianity. For some reasons she associated 'pagan' with 'Satanism' and refused to acknowledge that her God had not been silent all those centuries before Christ, but had revealed truths throughout the ages.

I saw the writing of the story of the Christian Saint Etheldreda as a way to show her, in images she would recognise, that my own belief in the Christ was as strong as hers, albeit expressed in a different way.

Before I had stumbled on Etheldreda at Ely I had known nothing about her. I do not remember ever having heard about her before that dramatic moment of contact. But once I started writing what I had 'experienced' in that hotel that night, she came into my life from several different directions.

There was a church near our house in South East London — All Saints in Lovelace Road. I had passed it hundreds of times and never entered. One day during the writing of my novel about Etheldreda I saw the door open and decided to look inside.

In the porch, pinned to a notice board, was an announcement that 'the healing group' would be meeting on Tuesday as usual. I stopped and read it again. As I had been walking along the road that day I had been thinking about what Dennis Barrett, the healer who had been instrumental in my recovery from angina, had said the last time I saw him. He said I should do healing work myself. This worried me because, of course, I wanted to do such worthwhile work, but had no confidence that I would be able to do it. 'Perhaps if I worked with a group,' I had been thinking at the very moment I noticed the door of the church was open and decided to go in.

'Wow!' I thought. 'What a coincidence!'

But the 'coincidences' did not stop there. As I came into the church I saw that it had magnificent stained glass windows. I had not yet started working with stained glass myself — that began in 1994 — but it had always been an interest of mine. I looked more closely. In the Lady Chapel at the side were several windows depicting female saints. One of them was Etheldreda! Another was Hilda, Etheldreda's contemporary and friend. On the other side of the nave were the male saints — Aidan and Cuthbert. The whole church seemed dedicated to the very Anglo Saxon saints I was featuring in my book.

For twenty years I had passed this church by. If I had come in at any time before this those saints would have meant nothing to me.

I felt incredibly moved, and knelt down and prayed.

For more than a year after this I attended the healing group in the Lady Chapel, kneeling beneath the image of Etheldreda. The sessions were very profound and very simple and we achieved a high rate of healing for those we prayed for. The vicar would read a line or two from the Bible and we would go into silent prayer in that beautiful, holy place. Then we would kneel at the rail and pray for a specific person we knew who needed healing, while the vicar laid his hands on our heads and prayed with us. From the first I felt that something profound and powerful was happening at that moment. It was as though we were enclosed in a ball of light and the vicar's hands became hot on my head.

The first evening I attended I was startled to hear the very verse read out loud that I had been 'given' at a séance when I was eighteen, a verse I was told would have great significance for me in my future life:

> 'Take no thought how or what ye shall speak: for it shall be given you in that same hour what ye shall speak. For it is not ye that speak, but the Spirit of your Father which speaketh in you.'
>
> Matthew 10 v.19.

I could not understand at eighteen what possible significance this could have for me, but when I became a writer and found that my best work flowed mysteriously as though helped in some way by an invisible presence, I wondered if that was what was meant. At any rate, that these verses should be read out now made me shiver. Surely something was at work here?

I began to attend Sunday services too, and for the first time since my childhood the Church began to mean something to me. When the vicar prayed he seemed to be praying to someone real, whose presence I could feel.

After some of the healing services we met for tea and discussion at the vicarage. There we examined such concepts as 'fruits of the spirit', which seemed to refer to the character of a person slowly maturing through life, and 'the gifts of the spirit' which was the sudden inrush of God's grace and spiritual help. Healing is 'His Gift' and was not reliant on our own talent — though our faith *could* make a difference. Another discussion centred on the long spiritual journey that made one ready for a miracle, and on the questions that should be asked: Do you really *want* healing? *Why* do you want healing? What are you going to do with your life if you are healed?

Although I look back on the time I attended that Healing Group as a time of continuous heightened spirituality, my diaries reveal many moments of inner turmoil and conflict.

I had been healed dramatically of angina after a visit to Dennis Barrett, a spiritualist healer in Bristol. I mentioned this to the vicar's wife, Thea, and she gave me a very stern lecture about seeking healing anywhere but through the power of Christ as manifested in the Church. She insisted that I give up any contact I might have with such persons and warned me that evil spirits might well attach themselves to me if I persisted. I tried to explain that Barrett himself believed in the Christ, but she would not listen. She stressed that the Church concentrated on 'making whole', the healing of a particular ailment being almost incidental. If someone was put in touch with the root of his or her being in the Wholeness of the Trinity, she or he would be made Whole and thereby healed in the deepest sense of the word. Whereas, if someone went to a healer outside the Church, they might well secure short term benefit and alleviation of symptoms, but the cause would still be there and the symptoms would more than likely return.

I tossed and turned in bed that night. Many people I knew who were healers outside the Church were beautiful, spiritual people. Most of my books were written about people who lived before Christ manifested on earth and yet spent their lives seeking, and very often finding, revelations from the highest Source. I thought about the Gnostics in the early years of Christianity who were condemned as heretics when the Church grew strong because they claimed that the individual could receive divine revelations direct from the highest source without going through the Church. I believe this — yet I do know Thea had made a valid point when she warned against reliance on imperfect spirits.

I thought about my own dramatic healing from angina. I trusted Barrett. He was a sincere and sensible man and he charged nothing for his services. 'It is not I who heal you,' he said, 'but Spirit.' I wondered what part The Christ had played in my healing. I had bought a silver fish pendant at Glastonbury on my way to see Mr Barrett, and when I had held it in meditation I had written 35 poems about the meaning of the ancient fish symbol in relation to Christ.

THE SIGN
An old man
on the doorstep
draws the outline of a fish
in the dust.
The tall passer-by
pauses.
Recognition comes
To each
In its own clothing
Of fire.
The wind blows the dust.
The fish loses shape.
But deep in the hearts
of the two men
the secret and eternal
message
swims on.

VESICA PISCUS
In the crossing of two circles
the Circle of God
and the circle of man

*the Fish
manifest itself.*

*THE INTERPRETER
I talk to the Fish
in my language
and He talks to me in His.
The interpreter
lives in a deep, quiet place
within me
and will not be hurried.*

*TO ALL DEPTHS...
To all depths
swims the Fish
in the ocean of Consciousness.
With Him
I explore
the secret places
of my heart
and find
the answer
to what troubles me.*

I had experienced something akin to spiritual ecstasy while I was writing the poems. Had this been what had brought about the healing, rather than the visit to Barrett? But I wouldn't have found the fish if I hadn't been on the way to Barrett, and my attention would not have been so focused had I not just left him. The spiritual journey making one ready for a miracle is a complicated and mysterious one. I was not convinced that it was only through a particular institution that Wholeness could be achieved. And what institution did she mean? The Anglican Church? The Roman Catholic Church? The Quaker? The Presbyterian? I had read the works of holy men in India and China who had not heard of the Christian Church and yet I believed they were more in touch with the Source of all Being than many clergymen I had met... It was true there was nothing to stop a person who believed in direct revelations from the Godhead claiming that God had commanded him to massacre a particular group of people, but the Church's record in the matter of massacring particular groups of people was not all that blameless.

If only one could be sure about the source of the revelations and insights one receives.

I have yet many things to say to you, but you cannot bear them now. When the Spirit of Truth comes, he will guide you into all truth...
John 16 v.12.

I, the Lord, search the mind and try the heart, to give to every man according to his ways, according to the fruit of his doings.
Jeremiah 17 v.9.

One evening I arrived at the Church for the Healing Service, very tired, but very cheerful and confident that the healing I was going to ask for my daughter's back would be granted.

The vicar prayed. The Lady Chapel was very quiet. I tried to compose my thoughts and stop thinking irrelevant thoughts.

Suddenly, and this is impossible to describe — I had a very powerful and frightening feeling. I was utterly and absolutely aware that God, and The Christ, *do* exist and was desperately ashamed of how we live in the world — the *waste* of our lives using so little of our potential.

I have wavered on and off all my life believing and not believing — but even my believing, compared to what I felt at that moment, was 'not' believing.

I was aware for the first time of what it would mean if the Word of God through Christ was *literally* true.

I started to weep and couldn't stop. I whispered to a friend to take the healing for my daughter.

She went up for the laying-on-of-hands and I stayed in my place and prayed — but I was in turmoil, tears streaming down my cheeks and my nose running disgustingly.

Later I tried to analyse my emotional response to that awe-inspiring revelation.

If what I had experienced was true I should 'give up everything' and 'follow Him'. But I did not want to! I wanted to continue writing books and poems, making batiks, having friends who were of all sorts of persuasion... and being close to Oliver who hates the Church...

At last I could not bear it any longer and, persuading myself that I must leave so that I would not disturb the others, I crept out, trying to compose myself before I reached home so that I would not have to tell my sceptical husband about it.

I did compose myself... made tea and watched television and pushed the whole amazing, magnificent gift of insight away from me.

If only, I thought, one could be a part-time Christian!

I did, in fact, continue as a part-time Christian. I don't believe 'The Christian Church' necessarily has the monopoly on Truth, but I hope and trust I won't ever deny or ignore the revelation of that particular night, or waste my potential completely. Writing is part of my potential, and I pursue that part with diligence.

Looking back, several poems I wrote at the time express something of the experiences that came to me under Saint Etheldreda's glowing image.

One evening the sermon concentrated on the problems of the nuclear bomb and how once it was invented, we could never escape it. The vicar stressed that it only destroyed physical matter — not spirit. The totally inadequate four-minute warning would not help us to survive the bomb physically, but was a perfectly adequate time for us to make peace with our God and survive spiritually. On the way home that night I composed the following poem.

No escape...
this hurricane of fire
is marked with our name
and will pursue us
to the end.
See now
the guiding candle flame
brighter than a thousand suns...
the ear
that could not hear before
hears now
the whispered Word
from which seed
the worlds were sown.
This is the Way,

*the Truth and the Life
inviolable
to our corruption…
the one true
last
remaining hope
when all is lost.*

After a particularly meaningful moment during the Eucharist I wrote the following:

*Twelve men around a table…
Twelve million fed
and more
who break bread
and drink wine
knowing suddenly what they do
and why they do it.
No academy
can teach as much —
or book
awaken so.
This is the Table of the Lord
where the food is Insight
and the drink is Truth.*

After a sermon on Eternal Life…

*No succession of days
Eternal Life.
No leaf fall
or harvest festival —
but a javelin
tipped with diamond
striking light…
the quick of the moment
with no end
and no extension.*

Walking home one evening I wrote…

The mighty power of angels
turns lead heart to gold.
The asking is the key...
and wanting... reaching...hoping.
Take now
this small and tarnished soul,
this creeping thing,
this dark and dormant seed...
Take and fling it in the air
where the great rush of wings
will blow it
to heaven's gate
and there
so work its alchemy
it will a proud thing be...
a shining
and a free...

But then the vicar left and another man took his place. The reality went out of the services. Even the healing sessions seemed to have become null and void. He prayed in a singsong voice and I felt he would have been shocked had Christ come walking into his church.

I left, and never went back, though I took away with me some important thoughts and memories. The dialogue between doubt and conviction continues in me to this day, but only about whether any institution, any group, or culture, has the true explanation of Reality. I never have any doubt about the mysterious different levels of existence — the visible beings and the invisible, the mind, body and spirit; the ultimate Unknown that lies behind the Known to which we all strive and of which we are all an integral part. I write story after story trying to understand this mystery — knowing that no construction of words can do more than hint, than point towards, can initiate a personal search on the reader's part... Each book I write is an exploration for me of the frontier between doubt and conviction, and so each book I write is a personal adventure.

Several years went by until I found a publisher for my novel about Etheldreda. The one I found had offices opposite Saint Etheldreda's Church in Ely Place, London. After my first visit to the editor I went inside the church to give thanks. Shafts of coloured light fell around me, and a choir at practice lifted my soul.

Another 'coincidence' pleased me. A friend, visiting my old home town of Pietermaritzburg in South Africa, told me that the maze in the nave of Saint Etheldreda's abbey at Ely in Cambridgeshire, England, is reproduced exactly in the new Pietermaritzburg Cathedral where I worshipped as a child. The maze has always been for me the symbol of search for spiritual enlightenment.

As ever when I write a novel I weave in my own experiences. In November 1978 I stayed in the guest room of my son Julian's College at Cambridge. I found it difficult to sleep, probably because as a young schoolgirl and student at Natal University I had longed more than anything to study at Cambridge. Here I was at St. John's College at last — living the life vicariously through my son.

In the small hours I got up and stared out of the window. Winter winds were tossing the black branches of the trees outside and it looked for all the world as though the full moon was caught in the branches.

I wrote the following poem:

Wild, the silver bird fought
the tree's black mesh.
Dazzle of feathers
as white fire sparked
in the flash
and the gleam of their fall.
The tree's blood-hold would not give.
The dark howled
with the wind's voice,
howled with the wound-pain
of the lonely traveller,
the lonely prisoner.
The tree strained,
creaked with the stress.
The cage of black and twisted sinews
could hold no longer...
gave
to the sky
the mighty wings,
the celestial spirit.

All night long it soared,
rode,
the moon in its splendour,
mocking me
who mistook illusion
for reality.

Years later this experience appeared, condensed, in chapter 1 of my novel *Etheldreda*:

'Penda's wolves are not God's children,' one of Egric's thegns shouted angrily. 'They are heathen and mock Him with their idols and their blasphemous ways.'

'A man standing in a field at night looks up and sees the moon caught in the branches of a tree. If he is wise he will know this cannot be, because the moon is immeasurably higher than the tree. It only seems as though it is caught, because he is standing where he is.'

'What has this to do with us?' Ethelhere said impatiently.

'The heathen are children of our God, no less than we, but *we* have learned that the moon cannot be caught in the tree.'

In chapter 4 of *Etheldreda*, my own childhood experience of walking on the beach on the south coast of Natal, South Africa was described in the following words:

Being a school attached to a monastery, there were not many hours of the day and night that were not accounted for in duties. But sometimes Etheldreda felt the need to be by herself and she would rise before dawn and, instead of going to the chapel where the monks and nuns would already be gathered, she would slip away to the sea and walk along the beach, watching for the sunrise. The air would be fresh and clear as though newly washed, the long beach curving to the distant headland pure and deserted. She would stand right at the water's edge, her sandals abandoned further up the beach, her shift gathered up and held above her knees, the waves washing over her feet, tugging at the pebbles.

At last the sun would rise, filaments and veils of light falling from it and floating away; she at the centre.

Later, in chapter 19, it was the contrast between the warm seas of the Indian Ocean and the cold grey seas of the North Sea off the east coast of England that made me write a passage that combined an experience I had as a child in the warm currents of Natal with one I had as an adult, in the cold currents of the Cape (South Africa).

Etheldreda removed her shoe and touched the water with her toe. It was freezing. The air was prickling with invisible ice.

She remembered the Irish monk Fursey from her childhood and how Hilda and she had tried to emulate him by walking in the snow with bare feet.

She took off her other shoe and threw them both back up the beach out of reach of the sea. Then she stepped into the water and gasped as her legs almost buckled under her with cramp. The sky blazed with sudden fiery brilliance as the sun came up over the horizon and a shaft of dazzling light shot across the watery leagues and drove like an arrow into her heart. She cried out and the cry was of a lonely child seeking its Comforter, its Counsellor, its Protector and Mentor.

Suddenly she felt no cramp, no cold. She found herself walking along the golden path that led from the beach to the sun, the air filled with singing and with a million sparks of light…beings swirled around her, bodiless yet recognisable to her in bodily form…It was as though all the barriers between the realms were down.

Eight

Stories of the West Country

I: *The Green Lady and the King of Shadows*

This story is set in Glastonbury in the Dark Ages.

Glastonbury is one of those numinous places around which myths and legends cluster — that the Tor is the haunt of Gwynn ap Nudd, an ancient Celtic god, challenged by the early Christians as a dark force; that there is a tunnel under the Tor; that there is a maze that can be traced on the sides of the Tor; that the Tor is a place for ancient rituals and a gateway to the Afterlife...

After I'd finished the first three books of *The Tall Stones* series, the character of Wardyke still intrigued me, and in the first version of *The King of Shadows*, started on 12 Jan 1978, I based the dark force that haunted Glastonbury Tor, on him. My publisher, Rex Collings, objected, saying it was a kind of cheating to have the same character recycled reincarnationally throughout all the books I wrote. Thinking he was to publish it, I gave in, and changed the name of the dark wizard to Gwynn-ap-Nudd, Lord of the Celtic Underworld, after a legend I had read about Glastonbury. I don't consider this "cheating" because I was describing an archetype, and archetypes, as we know, have many different names in many different cultures.

Because Rex was my publisher and he preferred to publish children's books, my first version had Lukas, the main protagonist, aged fourteen, like Neil in *The Weapons of the Wolfhound*, and Kyra in the first of the "Tall Stones" series. I had noticed that my own children took a leap in understanding at that age. One moment they were children and you could tell them what to do — the next you could not — they were thinking for themselves. I never caught the moment of change. But I was always astonished by it. I tried to express it in a poem I wrote when I noticed it had happened to Strat.

> *One day*
> *the boy looked at a Gainsborough*
> *and it was hanging on the wall…*
> *very big,*
> *very dark*
> *and very old fashioned.*
> *The next day*
> *he looked at it*
> *and it was all around him,*
> *the light caught him*
> *on the side of the face*
> *and glinted off the leaves,*
> *the clay was on his shoes,*
> *the twigs caught on his clothes.*
> *One day*
> *the boy looked at a tree*
> *and it was a thing to climb*
> *with a trunk and branches.*
> *The next day*
> *he looked at it*
> *and it was like a Gainsborough*
> *with depth upon depth*
> *of light and shade,*
> *richly beautiful.*

Later I read something that seemed to me to describe the different perceptions of people at different stages of development very aptly. A traveller finding men building, asked them what they were doing. One said: "Laying bricks." The second said: "Building a cathedral." The third said: "Honouring God."

Oliver illustrated the story in black and white. It was the first time we had collaborated on a book, and it meant a lot to me to have his drawings, though they were not as I saw the scenes or the characters.

Rex decided not to publish it, and for a while it lay in a drawer. But then John Matthews, a writer himself and a good friend, introduced us to Grahaeme Barrasford Young in Frome who agreed to publish three traditional Celtic tales I wrote, with illustrations by my niece Lynette Gusman. But he felt he could not afford to take on *The King of the Shadows*. Bitterly disappointed, we went away and thought about it, and eventually decided we would pay for it ourselves if Grahaeme would print it, as a gift to each other for our thirtieth wedding anniversary in 1981.

We spent happy hours driving from London to the West Country planning the name we were going to call our own little publishing company we now believed we should start.

As we lived in Dulwich, London, and it was "south of the river" while all our friends and museums and publishing houses were "north of the river", we decided to call it "The other side of the river" because, in London, that was a phrase often used. We thought this quite subtle as whatever side one was on, the other side was more unknown and mysterious.

Unfortunately, Grahaeme did not get the significance and the books were printed as being published by "The other side of the water" — which meant nothing to us or to anyone else.

The book looked very homemade. This was before desktop publishing with computers. But we loved it. It was our baby.

The story was based on several Glastonbury legends. One was that in the early centuries of the Christian era, a monk living on Glastonbury Tor, Brother Collen, confronted and challenged the Celtic God of the Underworld. Another was that there was a tunnel under the Tor in which a maiden had once been imprisoned. She became the Green Lady, the Spring Goddess.

We sold or gave away most of the 500 copies Grahaeme printed, and the book had another long sleep.

My German publisher, Neue Erde, published it, but he did not want Oliver's illustrations. A German friend Fred Hageneder, did a lot of etchings for it — but these were also not used.

I rewrote the book, making Lukas older, and rewriting the whole thing for older readers. I now called it *The Green Lady and the King of Shadows* weaving in more strongly a favourite theme of mine — the creative nature goddess and the destructive force that attempts to destroy her. In May 1978 Oliver had been sketching at Thetford, making illustrations for a book about ancient tracks in East Anglia by Shirley Toulson, and I had had a lovely experience on Thetford Mound which was covered with flimsy white lace flowers. I transposed this visionary experience to Glastonbury in the book (chapter 6) combining it with some of my thoughts on Glastonbury Tor during the time of the WESAK festival when I saw the moon rising at the same time as the sun was setting. It became the ritual union of male and female to renew the earth.

> It was then he felt her touch and a running line of fire seemed to spiral from it, burning the husks and stubble of his old self to clear the field for the new planting. With their limbs entwined they lay upon the earth and it was the pulse of the earth they matched with the rhythm of their lovemaking. No nectar could have been sweeter to a humming bird than that which flowed between them. A hundred, thousand people could have been crowding round them but they saw nothing, felt nothing, but the enclosing warmth of each other and the thrill that ran through every part of them
>
> The landscape was changing. All the scattered sheets of water were transformed into shimmering whirlpools of light, the marsh lands and reed beds, the dark trees of the forests — all seemed to have become spirals of energy. The slopes of the Tor were covered with white flowers like a bridal veil. Buds were visibly unfolding, branches pushing out new leaves. The young woman's bough had become white with blossom, emitting a dazzling light that shot out across the country bringing rich abundance to everything it touched. His own bare branch was covered with fresh green leaves.

In 1989 Jamie George and Frances Howard Gordon at

"Gothic Image" in Glastonbury contracted to publish the new version, without Oliver's illustrations, but with a cover by him. We had now moved to Bath because he had secondary cancers and it was predicted he would not live more than a year. We wanted a less stressful life than the one we had in London. He was to work for a few days a week as an editor for Gothic Image. He did a beautiful cover of angels hovering over the Tor, but the printer lost it, and he had to do another quickly on the day of the printing. I did not like this as much.

He died in November that year.

In chapter 10 of *The Green Lady and the King of Shadows*, Gwynn ap Nudd challenges the universe and tries to change it by the power of his will:

> He looked at the stars malevolently. He was sure the key he needed lay there in those vast stellar patterns.
>
> On earth he could change any structure at will. He could make clouds. He could lash the earth with storm and hail. But the key that made the whole function as a Whole always eluded him. He could change one thing but, in doing so, he disturbed something else, which then reacted in such a way as to make his first achievement at best null and void, at worst dangerous and destructive. The secret that kept everything in balance and harmony was still a mystery. He knew that if he made his final challenge, his supreme effort to change the universe so that all would be subject to him, without achieving this balance, he would destroy it, not change it.
>
> He came to believe that the stars held the key to the mystery.
>
> The ancients had studied the stars and had seen that they affected all that happened upon the earth.
>
> If he, Gwynn, could bend the motion of the stars to his own will, change the ancient configurations of the Zodiac and take the threads of its influence into this own hands, he could pull the universe to follow him and leave the invisible god, the disembodied god, the so-called source of love and harmony, helpless and defeated.

There is belief put forward by many people that the Zodiac is traced out on the land around Glastonbury Tor. It seems fanciful, but many a book has been written about it, and many a convincing map drawn. I suppose this was in my mind together with my own visionary experiences and my reading of books about magicians and shaman.

I had always been interested in John Dee who had lived at the time of Elizabeth I, but I had not read the following passage from the book *John Dee: The World of an Elizabethan Magus* by Peter J. French (pub. RKP, 1972) until after my book had been published:

> ...the religious magus could theoretically change the stars and control the heavenly powers. But the strain would be so great that his body would be destroyed and his spiritual essence would be completely absorbed into the Godhead. This great transformation was exactly what Dee was attempting through his magic.

II: *The Winged Man*

Even to this day in the ancient city of Bath there are images of Bladud — the city's legendary founder, who was the father of King Lear... the Winged Man. Restless at his father's court, a young prince sets off to consult a famous oracle. In this wild wooded place near a mysterious hot spring, the priestess proclaims he will become a great king, and one day fly like an eagle.

Returning to his father's hill-fort, Bladud's head is full of magnificent dreams... till trickery snares him in a loveless marriage. Embarking on an eventful journey to faraway Greece, he falls in love with a beautiful woman who already haunts his dreams.

Eventually Bladud comes home to find his wife and brother conspiring to disinherit him. Discovered to be suffering from a dread disease, he is exiled from court and disguises himself as a humble swineherd. Then, while he watches his pigs roll around in hot mud, a miracle is born...

When I first came to Bath in early 1989 I had never heard of King Bladud, but my interest in myths and legends soon made me investigate the local legend. His story attracted me mostly because he was not known for battles or for conquests, but for knowledge and enterprise. I was told he had founded the first healing sanctuary in Bath having been healed of leprosy by the hot waters that still well out of the earth here. I was told he achieved flight. I was told he was a sorcerer because he made fire out of stone. But when I heard he was the father of (Shakespeare's) King Lear, I could not but write a novel about him. I could not understand why his legend wasn't as famous as King Arthur's. It was every bit as exciting and inspirational.

My former editor at Arrow had now moved on to a relatively

new publishing company, Headline, and commissioned the book. I wanted to call it "King Bladud", but this was rejected and it was finally called *The Winged Man*, which, to me, was too vague and did not have the punch the first title had. Ideally, I would have liked the title, "King Bladud: The Winged Man".

Bladud was supposed to have descended from a line of Trojan Kings, and I found the ancient name for London was New Troy, Trinovantium. I puzzled about Trojans in Britain, but refugees are always moving about the world seeking asylum when their own countries are devastated by war or tyranny so why wouldn't the Trojans have done so after the Greeks had defeated them. There were stories of Trojan princes fleeing to Italy — Aeneas for one. His grandson Sylvius was killed by his own son Brutus in a hunting accident. Brutus fled to Greece where he married a Greek princess and then together they eventually sailed to Britain, landing, according to legend, at Totnes in Devon.

I visited Totnes and found the legend of Brutus alive and well there. I was even shown a boulder on which Brutus was believed to have stepped when he landed.

In Geoffrey of Monmouth's *History of the Kings of Britain* written in the twelfth century, I read the text from which Shakespeare derived his story of King Lear. There also I found King Bladud.

The story was buzzing in my head and everything seemed to be leading me to believe in it.

I visited my sister in Newark, not far from Lincoln, and her daughter drove us down a long straight road to Stamford for the day. We were wandering about the nice little town looking for a restaurant when we came upon the museum. Right in front of me at the reception desk were a few things for sale. I picked up a booklet on the history of Stamford and gasped as I read the name "Bladud".

It seemed that there was a legend that Bladud had visited Greece, many centuries before Christ, and brought back philosophers and founded the first academy, Greek style, at Stamford. I was tremendously excited. Meaningful coincidences were beginning to happen to me over this book as they had over the others I had written. I was on track!

I began to ponder the whys and wherefores and worked out a satisfactory explanation for why Bladud would go to Greece.

He was descended from a Trojan prince and a Greek princess. He might well have gone to "seek his roots" as so many Irish Americans do these days in Ireland, or black Americans do in Africa.

The next thing I pondered was how the Celts took to the Greek teachings, the two cultures being so different.

In chapter 17 of *The Winged Man* I examine the problem:

> The Greeks aimed to clarify everything — to leave no mystery.
>
> Everything must be examined, analysed, measured, categorised...Their method was principally question and answer, the students constantly prodded to provide rational answers, their answers in turn questioned, until they either broke down and withdrew them, or managed to uphold them under the gimlet scrutiny of their masters.
>
> The Druids, on the other hand, taught by means of a series of stories and metaphors: leading the students through a labyrinth of ancient myths and legends that were complex, mysterious, enigmatic, ambiguous, paradoxical. As the layer upon layer of rich, imaginative material built up in the students' minds, they reached a state of consciousness where suddenly the stories came alive and were experienced in such vivid form that a burst of illumination helped them to understand things never understood before.

Warming to the theme of the difference between the two cultures and the dichotomy within Bladud himself as a man of two traditions, I invented two women in his life, Rheinid the volatile and passionate Celt, and Alcestis the cool and caring Greek, between whom Bladud was torn. He loved both in different ways. My own experience of love told me that this was possible. That Bladud had a son was clear because we know about him, but his wife is unknown. Pondering on the fact that in Shakespeare's play King Lear is obsessively seeking love and obviously has no idea what true love is between parent and child, I thought that more than likely he would have come from a dysfunctional family. This was another reason I introduced conflict and division into the love life of Bladud and the home life of Lear.

The Winged Man is based on a legend and none of it might

ever have happened. But when a story is told often enough, and the Bladud story appears in many different texts throughout the centuries, it takes on a life of its own. To me — myths never happened in the ordinary world, but have a tremendous ring of truth as they resonate with human universal experience. But legends might have happened. Usually there is some figure at the start, a charismatic, powerful figure about whom rumours spread.

"Bladud is a sorcerer — he made stone burn!"

The modern researcher finds that coal seams exist very close to Bath where he was supposed to have made stone burn.

With enough sifting and examining and educated guesses a legendary figure emerges as a real historical figure.

I believe Bladud really existed and really did the things he was supposed to have done, and my mission in the book was to make him as believable to others as he is to me. But, because I also believe life is multi-dimensional, I have used powerful Celtic and Greek myths in the story to give it a different, deeper level of veracity.

When I wrote *Shadow on the Stones* I went into the question of early man being able to fly and could not see any reason why a primitive form of hang glider could not have been used. There were the stories of manned kites from China, and Daedalus and Icarus from Greece; even the Celts had their Druid Mog Ruith, who rose up into the air.

While I was writing *The Winged Man* I visited my daughter who was living and working in Rome. She had a boyfriend who lived in Naples and we planned to spend Christmas with his family. We hired a car and he drove us around to see the sights. One day he drove us to Cumae where there had once been a famous Sibyl, the very same Sibyl who had helped Aeneas, Bladud's ancestor, to enter Hades and commune with the dead.

I had never really thought about Cumae before, and hadn't asked the young man to drive us there. In fact, I had no idea it was nearby. There followed an extraordinary day — most pertinent to my writing that book at that time.

Not only did I discover that the area had been an ancient Greek Colony, so Bladud could well have stopped there on the way to Greece, but there was a plaque declaring that there was a tradition that Daedalus had landed there when he flew from Crete. I thought at once that may have been how Bladud got the inspiration to fly!

The day for me continued to be a day out of linear time, hugely significant for my book. That Aeneas had been taken by the Sibyl to the Underworld to converse with his death father, gave Bladud the idea to ask her to conduct him to the Otherworld to question Daedalus about flying. The description of the Sibyl's underground shrine and the landscape Bladud traversed to find the entrance to the underworld that Aeneas had used before in Virgils' magnificent epic poem, was the landscape I traversed that day with my daughter and her friend. I cannot tell you what a state I was in, slipping backwards and forwards through time, experiencing what I was experiencing superimposed on what I imagined Bladud had experienced. It was a most amazing, magical day!

Another very personal thing I wrote into the book was the "sky-stone" or meteor King Bladud found. One of my passions in life is astronomy and I have always, always longed to find a meteor that has travelled the universe. Just about this time my son Julian, knowing that I longed for a meteor, was telling an anthropologist in Venezuela about my writing. He asked him if he knew of a local shop where he might buy minerals and crystals and, possibly, a meteor. The man said he did not, but several days later came back to Julian and presented him with a piece of meteor as a gift, found locally. "If an author needs a meteor to access the infinite, she should have one," he said as he handed it over. My son gave it to me on his return to England.

In chapter 22, and later in the final chapter of *The Winged Man*, a meteor features:

> He clasped the sky-stone, turning it over and over in his hand, wondering about the Eagle King. How had he managed to fly. Was he borne up by nothing more than the magical power of his will? If anyone had the will to fly, surely he, Bladud, did? But the Eagle King was a man to whom the gods sent fire from heaven. What kind of mortal was that? A man who strides between the worlds with confidence; a man who believes in this world and in the next; who works with the other realms yet keeps his own strength and his own integrity. No slave, but a free man.
>
> 'I will fly,' Bladud thought — and then aloud, with conviction, he shouted: 'I will fly.'

III: *The Waters of Sul / Aquae Sulis*

In Britain, at Aquae Sulis, (present day Bath), hot waters gush ceaselessly from the earth. In ancient times the waters were associated with the supernatural.

In this novel it is 72 AD, and most of the country is under Roman domination. A rebellion is brewing in Aquae Sulis, the town under the protection of the Celtic Goddess Sul. The Romans have renamed her Sulis Minerva, and have tamed the steaming waters to form a complex of public baths.

Cults from Rome, Greece, Egypt and Judaea vie with the native Celtic beliefs and form a rich backdrop to the human dramas that unfold.

The Waters of Sul is set in a time of transition and adjustment, when beliefs are questioned and loyalties tested.

In the early 1990s I was living in Bath, North East Somerset, and my daughter Rachel was living in Rome.

I had never been interested in the Romans, seeing them only as conquerors and Imperialists and hating what I had read about their so-called "games" where people were torn apart by lions for the amusement of a bloodthirsty crowd. But I found myself living in a town in England that had once been a lively Roman centre for three to four hundred years and was proud to have the best preserved Roman bathing and temple complex in the country. I visited my daughter in Rome itself several times and it seemed to me I was soaking up so much Roman history, without even trying, that it became inevitable that I wrote a book about it.

My daughter loved Rome, but I did not. I remember one night she left me alone in her flat and I couldn't sleep. It seemed to me I could hear the screams and groans from the Coliseum and feel the terror and the despair of the victims.

But my interest in writing a novel set in ancient Rome was just beginning to intrude on my life, when "one of those things" happened that swung me over to writing about my own town instead, but in Roman times.

I was attending a lecture at Bristol University and during the interval browsed among the pamphlets and books on sale, I bought a copy of the Journal of Bristol and Avon Archaeology (1990/1991) and found an article on the remains of a Roman villa at Newton St Loe near Bath. It seems the villa was discovered during the building of the Great Western Railway in 1837. It was destroyed and would have been forgotten if a young engineer had not recorded it in his notebook. Now, more than a century later, James Russell, working from the engineer's notebook and sketches, gave a vivid picture of what it must have been like. The young engineer, T.E.M. Marsh, had also rescued some of the pieces of a magnificent Orpheus mosaic which are now displayed in the Bristol Museum.

I was fascinated, and not least because the place where the villa had been was well known to me. Just a short while before I had stood on the site where the farmlands of the villa must have been, investigating a crop circle. I still don't know what to make of these mysterious patterns that appear overnight in fields of ripening wheat, some simple circles, others complex patterns and glyphs. Some say they are made by hoaxers, others by artists practising a kind of landscape art. Many believe they are of extraterrestrial origin. I myself have pondered whether they are created by some kind of kinetic energy, set off by some powerful mind-link. It is certain we do not know all there is to know about the power of mind over matter, nor about the elaborate energies of the universe. But even if a man working with a plank and string is responsible for these extraordinary glyphs, it is still an open question as to what, or who, is influencing him to do this.

Whatever — I had stood in that pattern that warm, bright summer evening, feeling very strange, as though I was in the centre of a vortex of non-physical energy. Whether it was "just" my imagination or not, does not matter — this is how I was feeling, and this gave rise to the story I was to write set in 72 AD in Roman Britain. The villa the young engineer had described in 1837 becoming the villa of the Sabinus family.

Because of the mosaic of Orpheus I began to read books about the Orphic religion and found it quite close to my heart.

In my notes to chapter 4 in *The Waters of Sul*, published in 1998, I write about the Orphic religion:

Orpheus was originally a great hero of Thrace, possibly a king, distinguished for his wisdom and his musical talents, rather than for his warrior exploits. He was believed to be the son of Apollo, playing the lyre with such skill that beasts of the fields and forests, and even trees, gathered round him to listen.

When his great love, Eurydice, died from the bite of a snake, he journeyed to the Underworld and persuaded Hades and Persephone to allow him to take her back to earth. The only stipulation was that he was not to look back until they were safely out of the Underworld. Anxious to know if she was following, he looked over his shoulder — and lost her forever.

A Mystery Religion grew up around his name — featuring love and harmony between all beings. Texts believed to be songs and poems by him were closely studied. One of his most famous followers was Pythagoras (*c*.570–470 BC), a sage from Samos, who performed miracles and founded a centre at Crotona in southern Italy teaching Chaldean, Egyptian and Orphic wisdom. The Pythagoreans believed in reincarnation, and were vegetarian. They also believed with other followers of Orphism that mankind had inherited the guilt of their ancestors, the Titans, for which they were being punished by being kept prisoners in the flesh until they were "redeemed". They believed all, and not just "the gods", had immortality, but blessedness had to be earned. Pythagoras, like Orpheus, was believed to have completed a journey to the Otherworld while still in the body. The possibility of such a journey was therefore an acceptable tenet of their belief system.

Certain "golden leaflets" were found in tombs of the third century BC at Thurii, near Crotona, describing the Otherworld in vivid and beautiful detail.

Great philosophers who gained from and contributed to Orphism, such as Pythagoras, Heraclitus and Plato, broke away from the anthropomorphism of Greek religion and spoke of God as a spiritual power or energy. It was the mysticism of Orphism that led easily into the mysticism of Christianity and it was likely that St, Paul, succeeding with the Greeks where he failed with the Jews, was familiar with this mysticism.

There are several instances of floor mosaics throughout the Roman Empire that depict Orpheus, and behind him the chi—rho symbol which is made up of the Greek initials for Christ's name.

In chapter 11, I introduced my own experience in the crop circle as though it happened to Lucius Sabinus. Lucius became obsessed by wanting to visit the Otherworld as Orpheus had done.

In chapter 17 he persuaded Ethne to take him to Sul's sacred hill and there he attempted to pass through the gate to the Otherworld.

In the notes to chapter1 I place Sul's sacred hill in the present day context of Bath. When I moved to Bath I had no idea that a small extraordinary hill was within a few minutes walk of my new home. My sister Norma and I, exploring the district, found it, climbed it and stood on its summit surveying the amazing view that lay in a great arc below us. Above us several white doves flew round and round. White hawthorn blossom was everywhere. I was sure, though I knew nothing about it, that it was a very special place.

In the book I put a note about Sul's Sacred Hill:

It is known that the goddess Sul was worshipped on several hills around Bath in Celtic times. One, now simply called Round Hill, off Mount Road in the district of Southdown, Bath, rising above the southern ridge that rims the town, has always seemed to me a likely sacred hill. The view from the top is extraordinary. Glastonbury Tor, almost twenty miles away, is visible on a clear day, and I cannot believe that it has not been used as a special place since prehistoric times. It has more recently been used as a beacon hill, and sometimes, on Good Friday, three crosses in imitation of Golgotha are erected on the summit. Kelston, on the opposite ridge, was probably similarly sacred.

Later in this story I mention Solsbury. Please note this is not the same hill, but a much larger Iron Age hill fort to the north east of Bath, near Batheaston and Swainswick, now in the care of the National Trust.

Moments after my husband died my daughter and I climbed the Mount Road hill and stood on the top experiencing deeply profound thoughts about life and death. It was just after 4pm on November 1989 and the sky was the colour of a butterfly's wing — aquamarine and turquoise, one magnificent bright star poised above us. The valley and lands to the west seemed to be under mist and I couldn't help feeling that my husband's soul, like King Arthur's, was being ferried away through the mist to the Otherworld.

He and I had spent almost a whole night on the summit only a few months before, watching a total eclipse of the moon. Away from the streetlights and with the moon's light diminished, we watched the stars — millions of them. Knowing that he was soon to die, our yearning to meet again in the Otherworld was very painful.

In both my novel *The Winged Man* and in *The Waters of Sul* this little hill featured as a place of numinous power — an entrance to the Otherworld.

As usual when I write a book I think I am making up the story, but things keep happening which make me think I might be "tuning in" to something rather than just imagining it.

For instance, I chose the name Sabinus for Julia's family apparently at random because it sounded Roman. I had written the part of the story where I had Julia claim that she is the illegitimate daughter of the Emperor Vespasian when he was fighting in the district during the Roman conquest of Britain, before I read somewhere that Vespasian's family name was Sabinus.

I had made a major theme in the book, the disaffected Celts rebelling against the Roman occupation, before a visit to Cadbury Castle near Glastonbury revealed to me that the Romans had savagely put down a rebellion there in 70 AD. My character, Brendan, might well have fled from there to Bath to foment a second rebellion.

My story about King Bladud, *The Winged Man*, had been set circa, 800-500 BC when the legendary king was supposed to have ruled. By the time I was writing about in *The Waters of Sul*, this ancient descendant of the Trojans had already become a legend. There is a very famous Roman carving of a head found in the temple complex in Bath, but now housed in the Roman Baths Museum. It is traditionally known as the "Gorgon's Head". This had always bothered me as I had read in my Greek mythology that the gorgons were female, and this was unmistakably a male head.

I was sure it must be the head of Bladud and I wrote this into the book.

From Chapter 23 of *The Waters of Sul*:

At midday, Decius thought the work would never be completed in time for the festival, but before the late summer sunlight failed that night, it was in place. By half—light and flickering torchlight, he surveyed the pediment he had not seen complete before.

He wondered what the priestesses thought about having a male head upon their Temple. When first told, Bridget had strenuously objected but had quietened down when the whole scene had been explained to her.

Demosthenes had instructed the Egyptian well. Minerva's shield was at the centre as expected, but instead of a Gorgon's head to turn all enemies to stone, there was a magnificent male head. It was a combination of the British Bladud, the man who was believed to have mastered the art of flight, both physically and spiritually; and Aesculapius, the Greco—Roman god of healing. Bladud's wings and Aesculapius' snakes emerged from flaming locks that surrounded the mighty face like the burning flames of the sun.

Minerva's handmaids, Winged Victories, held the shield aloft triumphantly, garlanded with flowers and ripening fruits. Beings, half man, half fish, blew trumpets of celebration from the deep ocean, the mysterious realm of spirit in which we all have our being.

Two helmets were depicted, one with Minerva's owl of wisdom perching on its crest. Two spheres bound with thongs puzzled Decius for some time and then he thought they might represent the sun and the moon controlled by a great force beyond human comprehension.

It was a wonderful affirmation of the timeless power of

spirit that manifested through forms in time and space but was limited by neither.

One of the major themes in all of my novels is the search for a meaningful explanation of life, which usually takes the form of religion among the human race.

I am particularly interested in the confrontation of different religions. In my novel *Etheldreda* I had the Roman Christians confronting the Celtic Christians and both confronting the Anglo Saxon pagans. In the Egyptian novels there was the clash between Amun and the Aten. Even in the early Bronze Age novels, in the third, *The Shadow On The Stones*, there was the clash between the Temple of the Sun and the cruel god Groth. Here in *The Waters of Sul* I have the Roman state religion of Claudius, the God, the old Celtic worship of the Goddess Sul, the Great Orphic religion and the early Christian community founded traditionally by St. Joseph of Arimathea at Glastonbury. In 72 AD I knew there might be still people around who had actually met Jesus Christ and listened to his teaching.

I had crawled up Glastonbury Tor in 1976 when I was suffering from angina, on the way to meet the healer in Bristol who changed my life. Since my recovery I had been up the Tor many times, each time an experience of importance.

From the introduction to *The Waters of Sul*:

> The story of this novel is set in the late first century (*c.*72 AD), mostly in the town of Bath and its surroundings, but briefly also in Glastonbury, Rome, Pompeii, Petra and Jerusalem. The Roman name for Bath, in North East Somerset, England, was *Aquae Sulis*.
>
> By 72 AD the Roman invasion of Britain (in 43 AD) had settled down to an efficient occupation. Roads, temples and forums had been built, but the memory of Boudicca's bloody rebellion in 60 AD was still fresh in the mind, and there were still skirmishes between the Romans and the Celtic tribes.
>
> The hot waters that gush out of the earth at Bath, a quarter of a million gallons a day, have done so for millennia. The earliest people marvelled at the mystery and worshipped the gods and goddesses they thought were responsible for the phenomenon.

A potent ancient legend, well known in the region, tells of a British King, Bladud, who founded a healing sanctuary in the steaming marshlands when he discovered that the hot mud had curative properties.

By the time the Romans came, it was already a famous sacred place, under the protection of the Celtic tribe, the Dobunni and their Goddess Sul. Pilgrims came from all over Europe to take the healing waters and pay homage to the local gods. With their usual efficiency, the Romans tamed the waters, diverting them in lead pipes and drains to form a magnificent complex of public baths. They tamed the local gods as well, building temples to them Roman style, and giving them Roman names. The Celtic goddess Sul became Sulis Minerva and the town that grew up around the baths was called Aquae Sulis, the Waters of Sulis.

After the Romans left in the fourth century, their buildings fell into disrepair. An Anglo-Saxon poem of the eighth century describes the ruins:

"Roofs fallen, towers ruined;
Rime on the mortar,
Walls rent and broken,
Undermined by age.
As a hundred generations
Have passed away,
All who built and owned
Are perished and gone,
Held fast in Earth's embrace,
The relentless grip of the grave."

For centuries, the Roman town was forgotten until gradually bits and pieces began to emerge. The wonderful gilded head of Minerva so strikingly displayed in the on-site museum today was unearthed in 1727 when workers were digging a sewer beneath Stall Street. However, it was not until 1878 that the extent of the Roman remains was fully appreciated.

Today, many of the Roman buildings have been excavated and are on display, but many are still waiting to be discovered under the seventeenth, eighteenth and nineteenth century buildings of Bath.

How or why an author chooses to create certain characters

rather than others must have something to do with his or her own personal life. I write about twins because there were twin sisters in my family. I write about people fascinated with flying because my own brother, killed as Squadron Leader in the last World War, inspired me with his own passionate love of flying. So many of my heroines have red hair because two of my sisters had red hair and I always thought it was more beautiful than my own dark brown. I introduced an Egyptian into my novel about Bath because I am so interested in Egypt, but it turned out not to be as farfetched as it had seemed at the time. An Egyptian body from Roman times was found in a tomb in Walcot Street recently, and Walcot Street is where I envisaged my Egyptian sculptor's workshop.

When the book was published in 1997 it was published under the title *Aquae Sulis* which was the ancient Roman name for Bath. Waterstone's bookshop in Milsom Street did me proud, having the window totally stocked with my books tastefully arranged among Roman columns and artefacts. I gave a talk to a packed room. Wine was served. I felt really good, and was very hopeful that it would do well among the many tourists who came to Bath. It was mostly set in the complex of Roman baths and temples that are now preserved as the Roman Baths Museum.

I had come upon Martyn Folkes who had published the book in a manner that made me think our association was meant to be. Because it was a local book I was looking for a local publisher. Not knowing of any, I opened the phone book, and started phoning down the list of seven possibilities. As I went down the list I became more and more despondent. There wasn't a book publisher among them — mostly magazines and certainly not one that would even consider a novel. I was only going to try one more when I spoke to Martyn of Mushroom Publishing. He said "sorry" but he only published maps. I was about to ring off and throw the manuscript into the cupboard when he asked my name. Wonderful! He had heard of me! And we went on talking. It seemed he had been wanting to publish fiction for some time and decided then and there to consider mine for his first publication.

His wife Helen designed a beautiful cover for it — the Head of Minerva from the Roman Baths Museum on the front, with the Bladud head from the Museum on the back. Very Roman looking.

A piece appeared in the paper about it.

A few days later I opened my post and found a nasty, cold lawyer's letter saying that a certain man had the trade mark rights to the name "Aquae Sulis" for selling soaps and body lotions and I would have to remove the book from publication at once or pay him lots of money in compensation. None of us could believe it. The name was the name of Bath! How could anyone have given him exclusive right to it? I wrote a letter directly to him pointing this out and saying the publisher and I could not possibly pay. We weren't big rich people — but struggling to make a living ourselves.

His lawyer replied reprimanding me for appealing directly to his client and demanding withdrawal or payment immediately, quoting trademark law.

Friends and family suggested I take him to court because they were sure he didn't have a leg to stand on, but neither Martyn nor I could afford a court case either financially or emotionally. We both had sleepless nights, upset that anyone could be so mean.

I was getting sick with worry about it and employed my own lawyer to write a letter back. It cost me more than I could afford at the time. Meanwhile we noticed that a lot of the books had a fault in the binding, so we had to have them rebound. If we moved fast, we could have them rebound with a different title and cover. We decided to do this. We had to pay for the new cover, but at least he didn't get any money out of us.

The new cover by Stuart Littlejohn was good — but very different. The book no longer looked like a serious historical novel, but a fantasy novel. English Heritage who own most of the Roman sites around the country refused to stock it, as did the Roman Baths Museum in Bath — thus effectively shutting the door to the thousands of tourist sales we had banked on.

We both regret having given in. The new title *The Waters of Sul*, although a direct translation of the original *Aquae Sulis*, did not have the necessary punch, or tell the prospective reader that it was about the town they were living in or exploring as visitor.

In the 2007 edition, we have reinstated Helen Folkes' painting of Sulis Minerva on the cover, but have not risked using the original title "Aquae Sulis".

Nine

Non-fiction

Crystal Legends
Women in Celtic Myth
Myths of the Sacred Tree
Mythical Journeys, Legendary Quests
Three Celtic Tales

I have also written non-fiction books — collections of traditional myths and legends from around the world, grouped round a central theme, with commentaries on what they mean to me.

I believe with Carl Jung and Joseph Campbell that myth and legends are not just fantasy stories for children, but they are powerful expressions, in code, of a deep yearning towards an understanding of human existence; the human spirit seeking the truth about itself.

In *Crystal Legends* I explain why the current practice of "crystal healing" is based on crystal lore from ancient times, expressed through myths and legends which predispose us to believe that crystals have healing properties. Crystals and rocks have always fascinated me — from the time as a child in Drakensberg in South Africa when I hunted for agates in the streams, to the time I took a course of geology at University, and an evening course in paleontology in London in my forties.

I have never forgotten that we are living on a dynamic rocky planet hurtling through space in a magnificent universe full of wonders.

In *Women in Celtic Myth* I select eleven stories from the ancient Celts — from stories about formidable women warriors, to the beautiful companions of heroes, and tales of women who stand in their own right in the higher realms of spiritual wisdom.

In *Myths of the Sacred Tree* I have gathered together a collection of stories about trees reflecting a time when the natural world was deeply respected, and trees and forests were believed to be inhabited by spirits and divine beings. It is particularly apposite at this time to draw attention to the spiritual value of trees when we are cutting down the rainforests and endangering the whole planet spiritually and physically.

One of the most persistent themes in myth and legend in the world's many cultures is that of the journey — the quest. In *Mythical Journeys, Legendary Quests* I show the connection between the sacred journeys of myth and legend and the real journey of the individual soul towards enlightenment.

My search for meaning through these ancient tales has helped me considerably in my search for meaning in my life. They have lasted so well, and been told over and over again, precisely because they reflect human life so accurately, albeit in code. When you have deciphered the code, you have learned a lot about life.

Ten

Biography and Autobiography

I have written two other books that don't fit into my usual categories: a biography of my husband, entitled quite simply, *Oliver Z. S. Caldecott*, and this, my autobiography, entitled rather pretentiously, *Multi-dimensional Life*.

The biography came about because I believed Oliver to be a remarkable man, "larger than life" as a personality, a fighter against "apartheid" in South Africa, a courageous and interesting publisher in England, and a talented artist who deserves to be better known.

I knew his three children and six grandchildren wanted his life recorded, and his friends and colleagues might be interested to read about the man who had featured in their lives. But also his life story had something to give to the wider public.

The autobiography I wrote over several years, concentrating on the extraordinary things that happened when I wrote books. I finished it in 2001 and put it into a cupboard. I took it out again in January 2007, revised it and cut it down a bit for publication on my 80th birthday.

I am still ill at ease about publishing it — but I comfort myself that it is not just about me, but gives some insights into how a writer writes, and the complex thought processes that go on in people's minds.

About Moyra Caldecott

Moyra Caldecott was born in Pretoria, South Africa in 1927, and moved to London in 1951. She married Oliver Caldecott and raised three children. She has degrees in English and Philosophy and an M.A. in English Literature.

Moyra Caldecott has earned a reputation as a novelist who writes as vividly about the adventures and experiences to be encountered in the inner realms of the human consciousness as she does about those in the outer physical world. To Moyra, reality is multidimensional.

For more information about Moyra and her books, please visit www.moyracaldecott.co.uk.

Most of Moyra's books are available in both paperback and ebook. For more information, please visit www.bladudbooks.com and www.mushroom-ebooks.com.